"Little Black Girl Adventures is a touching and highly engaging personal story that gives children who have experienced trauma a starting point for healing. It provides insight into how your personal experiences do not define who you are but help to shape who you become! It is insightful and should be in all secondary classrooms and colleges!"

— Dr. Kimberly Bland, Chief Academic Officer for New Paradigm For Education

"A resounding standing ovation for Erica Robertson for taking the leap of faith to write *The Adventures of a Little Black Detroit Girl*! Her intergenerational readers will experience a love light in flight on the pages of this book and land with the belief that there is a little Black girl adventure in all of us. Erica has birthed a book that the world desperately needs right now, as she especially reminds young hearts and minds that there is a divine power and liberation to be discovered when we dare to share our stories."

—Shawn Dove, CEO of Campaign for Black Male Achievement

"The key lesson that all educators need to know about trauma is that there can be light at the end of the tunnel, and they can help be a guide to that light. For anyone who has experienced trauma or works with those who have, this is a must read to truly understand this journey must be taken one step at a time. Through Terri's journey, we are able to see the progression from pain to healing, rejection to acceptance, and hatred to love. She will make you smile, wince, laugh, and cry through her different adventures all the while making you proud and hopeful to the end."

—Christy Harris, Dean of the Relay Graduate School of Education

"Personal narrative is a powerful strategy and tool to reduce the impact of trauma for us all. More importantly, the ability to reclaim one's story is a form of healing that demonstrates resilience, the ability to overcome, and the courage to shift the discourse. This book offers great insight into the lived experience of the main character and is relevant to the lives of many youth in our communities. It highlights a nuanced illustration of personal discovery and reclamation. Youth would benefit from not only reading this, but finding ways to share their own stories."

—Karlin J. Tichenor, PhD, Founder and CEO of Karlin J & Associates; Co-Founder of Our Resilient Spaces

The Adventures of a Little Black Detroit Girl Homecoming

Dr. Erica Robertson

Little Black Girl Adventures
440 Burroughs, Suite 673
Detroit, MI 48202
www.littleblackdetroitgirl.com

Ordering Information:
Quantity sales. Special discounts are available on quantity purchases by corporations, associations, and others. For details, contact the publisher at the address above. Orders by U.S. trade bookstores and wholesalers. Please contact Little Black Detroit Girl Adventures: Tel: (313) 749-6257 or visit www.littleblackdetroitgirl.com

Printed in the United States of America

First edition: July 2020

Published by Little Black Girl Adventures. The Little Black Girl Adventures name and logo is trademarked.

The Adventures of a Little Black Detroit Girl author, Erica Robertson, provides speaking events. To find out more, go to www.littleblackdetroitgirl.com or call (313) 749-6257.

Some names and identifying details have been changed.

ISBN
978-0-578-72130-9 (hardcover)
978-0-578-72745-5 (ebook)

To my Heavenly Father, thank you for your love, your blessings, and your calling you have bestowed upon my life. Thank you for choosing me to do your good work.
I love you.

To my beautiful daughter Chloe, you are light, you are love, and you are loved. I am excited to see all the wonderful gifts you will share with the world. You are the inspiration that encourages me to share my story, you are the inspiration that encourages me to be a better me, and you are the inspiration that encourages me to help serve other little Brown and Black girls and boys. Thank you for being my inspiration.
I love you.

To my late mother Caldonia, you tried your best to give us more than you had. Thank you for instilling the values of hard work, education, and discipline. I am me because of you.
I love you.

To my late sister Monique, I saw your beauty and I saw your heart. You deserved more love than you were given. I miss you, Sister.
I love you.

To my loving brother Khary, you have kept smiling through it all. You are "love." Thank you, Brother, for sharing your love with me.
I love you.

To my wonderful cousin Mallory, you have always had my back. Thank you for being my rock in the midst of the storms.
I love you.

To my mentor, who told me I was the smartest young lady he'd ever met. Thank you for believing in me. You helped me fly. Thank you.
I love you.

Foreword

Alice Thompson
CEO, Black Family Development Inc

The experiences of this Little Black Detroit Girl transcend geography, age, and race. There is a place in the story for many of us as readers. A space to identify and heal from our own experiences of disappointment, confusion, consequences of wrong decisions, and traumatic experiences. But this book also provides a space for realizing one's hopes and dreams, resiliency, and vision for a better tomorrow. It is a must-read for young people of all ages.

The experiences of this Little Black Detroit Girl are about trauma, resiliency, love, friendship, and healing. It is about intergenerational trauma. The story is about the interruption of joy in a young girl's life, and how the interruption of joy can lead one to a distorted vision of one's self or one's future. This book is also about the hopes and dreams of a young girl that moved her to have a greater vision for herself and the courage to think and believe beyond her pain. This is a story of hope and recognition, and the fulfilling of one's purpose.

Kudos to Erica who, through this book, has touched the hearts of all of us who have shared in her traumatic experiences, albeit sometimes at a lesser degree. Erica shares how she moved from a traumatized little Black girl into a courageous, steadfast activist, educator, storyteller, and role model.

As I think about my personal and professional relationship with Erica, it is sometimes amazing to believe how much she has overcome to be the phenomenal woman that she is today. She is passionate for social justice, passionate for education, and passionate about her advocacy efforts to ensure that all children in Detroit have access to quality education. Her book tells a profound and courageous story of being an overcomer, refusing to wear the badge of victim, but rather embracing and walking in her victorious journey.

A Note from the Author

There I was, this fourteen-year-old skinny Black girl with big, frizzy hair I dyed red with a ninety-nine cent bottle of peroxide. I had on a pair of toothbrush-cleaned, white classic K-Swiss sneakers and a pair of oversized cut-off shorts I'd nabbed from my used-to-be best friend. I was sitting at the Greyhound bus stop waiting on my ride out of Austin, Texas. My ride far, far away from William Cannon Drive, the Summerville Apartments, and the neighborhood of Montopolis.

On William Cannon Drive there was the terror, fear, pain, and sadness of abusive parents. A sister who was kicked out of our house at fourteen and a brother who was taken away from us by Child Protective Services at ten. Later, in the Summerville Apartments, there was the loneliness and depression—countless nights in an empty apartment cooking dinner for just myself. And finally, in Montopolis, living with someone I thought was my best friend, but who instead used me, teased me, and left me to fend for myself without any money or family. I was waiting on my ride out of Austin, Texas, back to Detroit, Michigan, where I knew my grandmother's love would be waiting for me.

Today, twenty-five years after that trip to the Greyhound bus stop, I start my day the same way I do every day—with a cup of strong, black coffee and a receptive spirit, ready to give gratitude. The topics of gratitude vary day to day, but the one thing that remains consistent is my overwhelming appreciation for God's guidance, protection, direction, and transformative powers of love and faith. In my quiet moments of deep introspection, I am often drawn to Philippians 4:10 and hear Paul speak of being content no matter what, and I have truly grown to understand how that sentiment has shaped my life. And as my journey continues to unfold, my gratitude becomes that much stronger. For I, too, know what it is like to both be in need and to have plenty.

It wasn't until after my mother took her own life in July 2015 that I learned of her broken past. I knew she was one of seven girls, and I knew that her father was somewhat abusive. However, I didn't know the degree of the abuse until months after her death, when I sat down with one of my mom's older sisters. She told me that my maternal grandmother suffered physical abuse at the hands of my grandfather, her then-husband she married when she was just thirteen years old. I remember her telling me the abuse became so bad that my grandmother, who we all knew as Mother Dear, had to leave her girls for long periods of time to escape it and try to establish herself and a new place for them.

When the abuse from my grandfather worsened after Mother Dear's departure, four of the oldest girls decided to leave home. They ventured out on their own, found jobs and places to stay. The three youngest girls—my mother included—stayed behind. The abuse at the hands of my grandfather turned for the worse, and those three girls were physically, emotionally, and sexually abused.

When my mother was twenty-six, she had three young children: my younger brother, my older sister, and myself.

There was no father in the picture, and I would learn years later that there was a high probability we all had different dads.

We were living with Mother Dear on the East Side of Detroit, on Harding Street in a two-family brick house flat-trimmed in white and red that my grandmother had purchased some years after she broke free of my grandfather and reestablished herself. Two of my aunts also lived there—the two who had remained behind with my mother after the older girls left. Including my cousins, there were eleven of us there at the time.

I remember my mom leaving me and my siblings with

my grandmother for long stretches of time. I didn't quite understand then, but she said she was going out to get a job to help create a better life for us. She returned a year later with a new career in the Air Force, a new husband, and a new father for us kids, who legally adopted my brother, sister, and me. My mom packed us up and took us out of Detroit to our first stop on an Air Force base in Montgomery, Alabama.

Twelve years later, I was eighteen years old with a four-month-old baby and lived with my baby daddy Anthony, his brother, and his mother on the East Side of Detroit. I was on welfare, working two part-time jobs, and trying to raise my daughter. Like my mother, I decided that this life was not enough for me. I wanted my daughter to have more. I wanted to have more. I wanted to leave Detroit.

When my mom joined the Air Force, she got us out of poverty—and I had landed right back in it when I ran away from home at fourteen. But the military was an exit strategy, one I knew had worked for at least one woman. I told Anthony he should marry me, and I would go into the military while he finished college, and then he would support me through college once he graduated. Two weeks before leaving for boot camp in Great Lakes, Illinois, and eight days after I married my daughter's father, something terrible happened. Anthony killed a man and went to prison. At eighteen, I left my daughter with Anthony's mom, and went out to the military to try to figure out how to create a life for my family.

Three generations of women tried their very best to provide a better life for their children. Women who escaped their meager, desperate, and often terrorizing circumstances and journeyed out in the world alone armed only with hope, faith, and determination they could build something more for their families than they had for themselves. All of whom returned, as they had promised their children, with more financial stability and a future filled with opportunity and optimism that there was more to life than their current circumstance; all of whom returned with emotional and psychological trauma from their earliest experiences they worked hard to escape, but still battled with the scars.

Intergenerational trauma is real. I'm still learning about the link between the historical trauma and racial terror my grandfather must have experienced as a young Black man growing up in the South, just one or two generations post-slavery—and how those traumatic experiences shaped how he treated my grandmother. But what I do know a little more about is how this form of post-traumatic stress disorder, if not treated and cared for, can haunt generation after generation.

This is my story.

It is a love story.

It is a story of transformational love.

The transformational love of God.

The transformational love of a someone who believed in me with his whole heart.

The transformational love that comes with the courage to love yourself.

And it is about the transformational love of commitment to more than just yourself.

This book is based on true events from my life. In it, I take on the character of Dr. Theresa Erics, PhD. Some names have been changed, some events, organizations, and characters are fictitious to keep identities private. However, I feel that I must tell my story. First, to continue the healing journey I've been on for the past twenty-plus years. Second, to help my daughter on her own transformational journey to peace, health, and happiness. Third, to encourage, support, and inspire other young Black boys and girls who have had similar experiences that there is hope for tomorrow. You can find joy, peace, healing, and happiness for your future self—even if today hurts.

Prologue

Great meeting today. Here is the article we discussed over breakfast with the Transportation Chair. Let me know your thoughts.

TERRI SAW THIS TEXT MESSAGE FLASH on her iPhone as she sped right past her house. She often found herself completely lost in thought, too distracted to notice she'd already made it home. She put the car in reverse, then backed into the driveway of her brick colonial home, which was originally built in 1927.

Terri loved her house. Prior to moving back home to Detroit, she had only rented as she didn't want to be tied down. She was a bit of a gypsy, living all over the United States—except for the last ten years she spent living in Paris, France. She had finally decided to take root and commit . . . to a house at least.

Terri reversed up the driveway past her wide front porch that spanned the width of the house. Every time she would arrive home, that porch felt like an invitation to relax. Terri spent most spring and summer mornings on her porch with a cup of black coffee, her Christian R&B playlist crooning on her iPhone, the early edition of the *Detroit Free Press*, that day's *New York Times*, and the latest spiritual development book in her lap. This season she was reading *Secrets of the Vine* by Bruce Wilkinson.

She could relate to Wilkinson's analogy of God as the "vine dresser," both in the Biblical and literal sense, as she fancied herself a bit of a gardener. Each morning, as a part of her routine, she would come out to prune her bright red geraniums. Just last week they'd reached a gorgeous full bloom. She was particularly in awe of these magnificent flowers because for a short while, she had gotten too busy to prune and water the flowers and they had withered. But Terri knew with love, meticulous pruning, and watering, the flowers would come back. This also applied to Terri. There were seasons where she would get so busy, she would deprioritize her spiritual nourishment and her spirit would wither a bit, but she learned that with meticulous weeding, pruning, and watering she would come back to full bloom—just like her geraniums.

As Terri pulled past the flowers, she let out a deep sigh of relief, grateful she was finally home. It was a Friday night, and Dr. Theresa E. Erics, PhD was officially off the clock *and* home before dark—a rare occasion. She always had commitments to work functions, which were important, but she felt blessed when she could get home before the streetlights came on and grab a little Terri time.

Today had been intense. Terri had arrived in Lansing at 8:00 a.m. that morning after a ninety-minute drive from her home on the west side of the city. Monday through Friday, Terri was up by 4:00 a.m. She didn't need an alarm clock anymore; she had just grown accustomed to early rising. Terri was at her best early in the morning. She spent an hour in deep meditation and Bible study, an hour working out either in her home gym in the basement or at the fitness center around the corner, and another hour getting ready: taking a shower, doing her hair, and drinking a green smoothie drink. Today, however, Terri had to cut her routine short because of an early meeting.

Terri had convinced her hairdresser to pop in early that morning. She had been working out intensely and steaming the last few days, and her hair had gotten a bit unruly so she wanted her hair to be on point for that day's many meetings. Terri had a long, sandy-red mane, with a chic, U-shaped cut that was always neatly and conservatively styled with a swoop bang in front. Terri had dark, sparse freckles that accentuated her high cheekbones, bronzed skin that looked like she'd been kissed by the sun year-round, and a smile that lit up any room. Terri was totally oblivious to how strikingly beautiful she was, but she always kept herself neatly groomed and in high fashion.

Today, Terri had decided to wear a pair of black Escada cropped trousers and a nude silk Eileen Fisher sleeveless blouse that peeked beneath a powder-pink Theory blazer. She adorned her lips with a light-pink shade of Volupte Rouge Yves Saint Laurent lipstick and powdered a YSL blush on her cheekbones to match.

She called her powder pinks her "power pinks." Terri was a feminist but did not fall within any one definition of the ideology. Terri believed that living her truth was the most authentic and powerful form of feminism, and every woman possessed their own unique brand. And to Terri, social justice, service to others, spiritual enlightenment, and a pair of Christian Louboutin Red Bottoms were her forms of feminism. Terri had learned later in her career that embracing her feminine side in male-dominated industries was the true expression of feminism and power.

Her first meeting had been a working breakfast with her colleague June Lee, Chair of the of Transportation Committee. They had met at one of Terri's favorite spots in Lansing, the Grand Traverse Pie Company. Terri sat on the Regional Transit Authority Board, among many others, as she was committed to supporting her city and her people.

The upcoming year was a big one for the RTA, as they were pushing to get their mass transit initiative back on the ballot. The last time it had been up for a vote, it failed by a slim margin. This time, however, the RTA had planned a strong ground game to engage young people, seniors, and people with physical disabilities who counted on public transit every day. All that was left to do was push a piece of legislation through that would ensure the initiative could go on the ballot. Terri was extremely passionate about transportation and fearless while working on behalf of kids in Detroit.

Terri had come a long way since being a girl in the city herself. Terri got pregnant in high school, and soon after graduation, at eighteen, married her high school sweetheart and the father of her child, Anthony Rivers. Eight days into their marriage, Anthony got caught up hanging with his friends in the streets and took another man's life. He went to prison. This was an unfortunate and all-too-frequent occurrence with the young Black boys in Detroit, which left the young Black girls to figure out how to manage on their own.

Anthony, his mother Verna, and a pregnant Terri lived under one roof on the deep east side of the city on Coplin Street off Kercheval Avenue. Anthony and Terri were getting by on Terri's two part-time jobs—one at a Perry Pharmacy and another at a Kentucky Fried Chicken—Anthony's job at the gas station, and Women, Infants, and Children (WIC) vouchers and food stamps from the state. Today, she was the CEO of Our Black Boys Matter, a non-profit focused on challenging racial and economic injustice and protecting, promoting, supporting, and educating young Black boys in her city and one day, she hoped, nationally.

She managed to break free from the hardships of her adolescent life by the grace of God, the values of discipline and strength her mother instilled in her as a child, and a few amazing people she met along the way. But for many of her friends, that life—the life of single parenting, minimum wage, state assistance, and, in most cases, poverty—had a tight grip, tough to loosen, and for many of her high school friends, it remained their reality. Terri wanted to spend the second half of her career helping change that narrative for the young people in her city.

The next meeting had been a late lunch at the Rattlesnake Club, right across the street from her office on the other side of town. Terri was speeding down the Walter P. Reuter Freeway, headed back to Detroit, bumpin' some Cardi B in the background. She heard Cardi's lyrics:

I was in the field, man, I slaved for this.
Had to talk to God, dropped down, and prayed for this.
To my surprise, He replied, said, "You were made for
this."
I'm living my best life . . .

As she was feeling each verse of that track, she reflected back on her first time at the Rattlesnake Club. She was twenty-two years old, still in undergrad at the University of Michigan-Ann Arbor, on a date with Roger Mason. The Rattlesnake Club was the fanciest restaurant she had ever been to in her life. Back then, the Rattlesnake had everything she wanted in her life: the glamour, the power, the romance. Now, a modest grin spread across Terri's face as she compared her life then to now. She felt nostalgic. Although the Rattlesnake remained a symbol of success in her mind today, it was more of a convenient spot for lunch meetings. Terri now dined there two or three times a week. All the waiters knew her by name, and the general manager Dina, always had a little something special prepared for her when she'd have guests.

She had pulled up to the valet and stepped out of her car. She had strode into her meeting with Dr. Lola van Belle, Provost of Diversity at Wayne State University; Ralph Blonde, the CEO of the National Society of Social Justice for Young Boys of Color; and Tiffany Thomas, Vice President of the Urban Alliance of Teachers. They had spent the afternoon brainstorming a few innovative ideas that could help inspire and support young Black boys and reengage them in school.

At home, Terri snagged her to-go box from Gregg's Pizza and BBQ and her four pack of Perrier out of the back seat and slammed the car door. Kicking off her heels as she entered through the garage, she drank in the splendor of her living room. Her fifteen-year-old Pier One brown leather love seat was calling her name. She sank into the couch with the to-go box of barbecue in her lap and cracked open a Perrier. Terri preferred wine with dinner but had decided to give up alcohol for twelve months as a part of a cleanse. The cleanse, however, said nothing of the occasional slab of beef ribs.

Terri was a beautiful walking contradiction in so many

ways. She loved that about herself. Because of the life Terri had, the many places she lived, and the people she interacted with, Terri had become a gorgeous collage of her many experiences. And on this night, she was a collage of beef ribs, half a pint of Häagen-Dazs butter pecan ice cream, sweatpants, and *Frasier* queued up on Netflix.

Terri relaxed; her feet propped up on her ottoman. Out of the corner of her eye, she saw the screen on her iPhone light up. She decided it would have to wait until Monday. She closed her eyes for a moment, took a deep breath, and gave gratitude that she was now living her best life.

Part 1
You Love Me? How Can That Be?

1

Side by Side

Just getting out of bed. Are you there yet?

TERRI SAW THIS MESSAGE POP UP on her phone as she made her way up Woodward Avenue, heading to LA Fitness. It was a message from her twenty-six-year-old daughter, Zoe. Every Saturday Terri would rush to the gym at 8:00 a.m. ahead of Zoe to reserve two bikes for the 8:45 a.m. spin class. Terri always wanted to be the first one there so she could ensure she and Zoe could get bikes next to each other.

She was excited to meet Zoe at the gym as this was a somewhat new routine the two of them had committed to over the summer. Terri was so grateful that they had a close relationship now, because as a young parent, she knew she had made a few mistakes raising Zoe. And Zoe had rebelled in ways that were hurtful to Terri. Given the complexities of their past, Terri wasn't naive in thinking the relationship with her daughter was now perfect, but she woke up every day with an overwhelming sense of gratitude that she had more time with Zoe to demonstrate her love in a healthy, nurturing, and encouraging way.

Terri didn't have regrets about her past mothering. She'd learned along her journey that regrets are useless emotions tied to guilt, unforgiveness, and shame. Instead, she chose to use those experiences of her past to help other Black families. In Terri's studies around social justice, she had recently come to learn about Post-traumatic Slave Syndrome, an epidemic she now could clearly identify after reading a thought-provoking book by Joy DeGruy-Leary, PhD. In her work, Dr. DeGruy explains how the injury and trauma from slavery has been passed down through the generations, and how this epidemic has negatively impacted the Black family unit and contributed to unhealthy parenting behaviors and practices.

This concept hit very close to home for Terri. She felt her fight for social justice would be incomplete without addressing this cultural poison that had wreaked havoc on Black families. It had devastated her own family growing up and almost had destroyed her relationship with Zoe. Terri knew she was taking on very big, very deep, very heavy emotional issues, but she couldn't fathom trying to break the cycles of intergenerational poverty and heal the socio-cultural fabric of her community without first trying to heal her own family.

Calinda, Terri's mother, always blamed her and her siblings for limiting the opportunities she had missed out on in life as a young mother. Terri believed the exact opposite about her own daughter. It was because of Zoe that she'd had an amazing career. Zoe had forced Terri to not only be responsible at an early age, but also confront her trauma and try to be a better person for herself, for her daughter, and for her community.

It had taken some time for Terri to truly appreciate how grateful she was for Zoe. For years she'd carried the shame of being a teenage mother. Terri felt she had to prove to the world that she was worthy, even though she had gotten pregnant at sixteen. She had to prove to the world that she was good enough to be successful. The thought of not being successful did serve as a motivator, but more so was the debilitating fear that caused her overwhelming amounts of anxiety. Anxiety had robbed her of the joy and her happiness of being a mother when Zoe was a child.

After years of hard work, Terri had now achieved a level of peace and joy she'd never thought possible. She loved herself and she loved life. And, most importantly, she could now express a different type of love to her daughter. A warmer more affectionate kind of love she knew Zoe had needed more of when she was a child, yet still wanted as a young adult.

The only love Terri had available to give when Zoe was a small child was that of a provider. Love, to Terri, was ensuring Zoe had three nourishing meals a day. She'd learned that from her mom and stepdad, K.C. Terri's childhood and home life was traumatic and chaotic, to say the least, but she always had three meals a day and dessert once a week (if she demonstrated good behavior). Not too much dessert though, because her mother Calinda didn't want her children "getting fat," as she would say—a parenting behavior Terri had also picked up from her mom, one which had caused a lot of stress for her and her sister Nikki as young women, and later for Zoe, too.

Terri had always seen herself as fat, and she developed an eating disorder in her twenties. During that time, Terri was five foot seven, 120 pounds—a decidedly healthy height and weight. But she'd been obsessed with her body. The intense fear of being fat she'd acquired from her childhood, plus living in a time where super-thin was a necessary component in "making it" in a mainly white, mainly thin corporate culture had continued to fuel Terri's fears and anxiety, both of which she worried she had handed down to Zoe.

However, Terri had learned to manage her obsession with weight and to back way off Zoe on that issue, and she now allowed Zoe the space to walk her own journey. She just wanted Zoe to be okay and to be comfortable in her own skin. She wanted Zoe to achieve a high level of confidence earlier in her life than Terri had been able to.

It had taken Terri years of therapy and self-work to develop a healthy sense of self. She remembered walking into a therapist's office when she'd first entered the Navy at the age of eighteen. The therapist asked why Terri was there. Terri had responded, "Because I don't want to be like my mom."

Terri had been seeing counselors and therapists regularly for the past fifteen years now. When she'd started therapy, Terri knew she had a lot of hurt places, but she had difficulty identifying them. She knew her hurt was spilling over into her relationship with Zoe, but she didn't know how to stop it. She wanted so badly to be a good mother.

But because the wounds had been so deep, so fresh, and Terri had been so young, she did carry much of that trauma into the relationship with her daughter when Zoe was little. The constant fear of failure in a world that already saw Black as inferior and the psychological and emotional trauma from her own childhood had kept Terri off balance for much of her motherhood. She could not name it as clearly then, but she now understood the impact of raising a child while struggling with her own psychological and emotional injuries. Because of those experiences, Terri now felt compelled to help other young mothers and families in her community. She could relate without judgment, but with compassion, understanding, and humility.

As Terri turned into the gym parking lot, she pulled herself back to the present moment. She got out of her car, moved swiftly up the stairs, and into the gym. She was the first person in the spin room, and she had successfully secured two bikes for the spin class, one for herself and one for Zoe—side by side.

2

No Simple Questions

WHEN TERRI AND ZOE FINISHED THEIR spin class, they sealed their workout with a relaxing hot steam at the gym. Then they went for lunch in one of their favorite brunch spots, One-Eyed Betty's. One-Eyed Betty's was a hip little American-style pub in Ferndale, a trendy city just north of Terri's home in the University District. Zoe ordered the Ridiculously Good Grilled Cheese, as it was famously named, and Terri ordered the pork belly poutine. Both were fully aware they were putting back on double the calories they burned at the gym, but it was worth it.

As the two were chatting, sipping on their sparkling waters, and waiting for their lunch to arrive, Zoe asked a very interesting question out of the blue.

"Mom, how would you feel if Dad wanted to get back together with you once he gets out next January?"

Tony, Zoe's dad, had served twenty-six of his twenty-five to thirty-five–year sentence he received for manslaughter and was due to be released the following year. Zoe had just been eight months old at the time of his incarceration, but Terri made sure Zoe remained in close contact with Tony and his family as she grew up. Terri would take Zoe to the prison regularly for visits. Depending on which prison he was in, sometimes the drive would take up to four hours one way. Terri very much disliked bringing her daughter to a place where she had to be frisked, where Zoe had to see her father in a prison uniform. However, she understood the importance of the bond between daughter and father, and she knew how much gratification Tony received from seeing his daughter.

Tony was now in a prison closer to Detroit, the St. Louis Correctional Facility, in St. Louis, Michigan. It was a Level IV prison that included very lenient rules, but also substantial pre-release preparation, like psychological counseling and academic programming.

Terri paused before answering Zoe. She wanted to give a thoughtful response. Terri didn't know what Zoe was thinking, so she wanted to be careful not to crush her daughter's spirits.

Terri first tried to deflect. "Yes, I am excited your father is getting out of prison soon! He is still a young man and has the opportunity to use his experience to help other young men in the next chapter of his life—"

"Mom," Zoe interrupted.

"Oh, your question," Terri said with a small grin on her face. Her daughter was too sharp and too grown for the sloppy sidestep.

"You know Zoe, when your father went to prison, I was eighteen. I was a child. And he was barely twenty. It will be twenty-seven years we've been apart. We have grown in two vastly different directions. And you also know that I love Jean-Marc."

"Yes, Mom, I know. I like Jean-Marc for you, but would you be torn?"

"Listen, baby doll. I love and care for your father a great deal. He was a friend to me when I needed a friend and he took me in and he cared for me. And I will always love him for that. But it's a 'philia' love, the type of love you have for family members," Terri said.

"But you once loved him romantically, didn't you?"

"You know as I've gotten older, I realize that at fifteen or sixteen, sometimes you think you are in love—romantic love—but there are so many other factors at play. And you know that is still true when you are older." Terri winked.

"Mom!" Zoe said and chuckled. "Why can't you just answer a simple question?"

"Is it a simple question?" Terri quipped back, jokingly. "Okay, I tell you what. I will tell you our story. The story of Tony and Terri. And you tell me if it's a love story. Cool?" Terri looked at Zoe for permission to proceed.

"All right. I've only heard bits and pieces from both you and Dad. So this should be good," Zoe said, wide-eyed. "But please, do me a favor, Mom, and leave out any sexy stuff. I so do *not* want to hear that," Zoe added with a giggle.

"Yes, Zoe, you were delivered to us wrapped in a pink blanket in a basket delivered by a stork," Terri teased as they broke into laughter, both with the signature family snort sprinkled throughout their laughs.

As Terri began to tell Zoe her love story, Terri vividly recalled her first encounters with Tony . . .

3

Coach Put Me In

ANTHONY RIVERS PLAYED CENTER FOR Southeastern
High School boys' varsity basketball team. He was a senior,
and Terri was a sophomore when they first met in Home
Economics. It was considered an "easy A" class because all
you learned was how to take care of the home—still, Terri
learned some valuable skills. She learned how to create a
home budget, prepare some basic meals, and even take
care of a "flour bag baby." Anthony was her husband in the
flour bag baby routine.

Anthony, or Tony, was a kind and easygoing tough
guy from the East Side of Detroit. His skin was a beautiful charcoal black—so dark, he had the nickname Smoke.
Terri developed a crush on Tony as they cared for their
flour bag baby. At first, she was little turned off by his blue

jumpsuit Dashiki he would wear every third day, but who was she to judge? She wore the same oversized "borrowed" pants at least three times a week.

After their project was finished, they continued to bump into each other in the hall. Terri fell for his loud laugh, wide smile, and lighthearted sense of humor. Tony also had this quiet strength about him; he was well respected at school, and Terri felt safe with him.

When Terri started getting to know who's who at school, she found out Tony was in a gang, and it strangely made her feel even safer with him. Since moving from Austin back to Detroit to live with Mother Dear at fourteen, Terri felt she needed to make friends who could protect her. She had a few run-ins with some young ladies from the job corps on her way to school and a few "accidental shoves" by her locker in the hallways. Terri tried to hold her own, but wanted someone who could help look after her, keep her safe on the streets, and in the school hallways. Tony could be that friend for her.

But Terri wanted to be more than just friends with Tony. To solidify her intentions for Tony and earn his attention, Terri decided to join the Jungaleers Junior Varsity girls' basketball team. But joining the team was more than a ploy to get a boy for her—she wanted to be a part of something at school. She wanted to belong. Terri didn't know much about the game—she had been a cheerleader before leaving her high school in Austin—but she did know the boys' and girls' basketball teams hung out together, and that was reason enough for her.

Terri was horrible at tryouts. She couldn't land the ball in the hoop, she couldn't dribble, she didn't know how to pass. Heck, she barely knew how to hold a basketball. But for whatever reason, the coach of the basketball team really liked Terri. Coach Rub saw Terri's charisma, her boldness, her courage as she went after something she wanted even if the bar was extremely high. Terri truly believed that if you wanted something, you should go for it. If it doesn't work out, at least you tried.

It seemed like Coach Rub could sense that Terri wanted to be a part of something—that she *needed* to be a part of something. So he gave her a spot on the team and brought her into his community.

She never got much playing time, but Terri came to practice every day. She suited up for every game, she traveled to every away game. Terri used to be a loner, but now she felt she was a part of something. She felt she had friends who liked her, and she felt special.

Normally, Terri was fine with not playing. She knew she was no good at the sport. But on their last game of the season, Terri wanted her turn on the court. She really wanted to contribute as a team member. She had formed a bond with girls on the basketball team, and she wanted to be part of their winning season. And more importantly, she wanted her teammates to be proud of her.

"Coach Rub, Coach Rub! Put me in," Terri called from the bench.

Coach Rub turned to Terri and put his hand on her shoulders.

"Terri, I don't want you to embarrass yourself. Now sit there and be quiet."

Terri raised her eyebrows and folded her arms, ready to pout. But she quickly realized he was right. If she went in the game, she'd let her team down.

She did, however, achieve her objective of becoming Tony's girlfriend. Terri attended all of Tony's games and cheered for him; she was his personal cheerleader. He was an amazing point guard, so swift and in control down the court. After each win, the girls' basketball team would go to the pizza place or Coney Island restaurant with the boys' team. And each time they'd go to dinner, Terri would sit by Tony at the restaurant. She would eat off his plate; that was her way of flirting. It was also her way of gauging if he liked her. In her mind, if Tony allowed her to eat off his plate, that meant he was into her. If he was offended or gruff, that meant the opposite. He didn't mind and in fact, he became accustomed to Terri picking off his plate. Whenever his food arrived, he'd push it close to Terri so she could take what she wanted. On the nights he noticed Terri didn't have money to order her own food, he'd order extra so Terri could have enough to eat.

Terri also attended Tony's practices when they didn't conflict with hers. She liked watching him play ball and horseplay with the other guys on the team. Tony was such a nice guy, all the players on the team liked him. And they all liked her. They knew there was something going on between Tony and Terri. And if you were a friend of Tony, you were a friend of theirs. The boys' basketball team became like Terri's brothers. They would tease Terri sometimes.

"Terri, are you taking notes here?" Derrick, the team captain, joked. "Maybe if you picked up some of our moves, Coach Rub would let you play." The whole team cracked up. Even Tony laughed. But it was okay, Terri knew they joked about her because she was one of the gang.

One particular evening after practice, Tony asked Terri if she wanted to come over for dinner.

"Hey Terri, Mama's cooking wings for dinner. You want to come over?"

Before Terri could respond, Tony added, "Yeah, Mama asked me to invite you. She said you called so much she wanted to see who you are."

Terri blushed. She knew she called Tony all the time. And when she wasn't calling him, she was waiting by the phone for him to call her. She really liked him, and she felt he liked her too.

"Whatever!" Terri replied, rolling her eyes at him.

"Whatever!" Tony mocked her accent. Tony and all the guys on the basketball team always teased her about sounding like a white girl.

They both laughed, and Terri hit Tony on the shoulder.

"Shut up," Terri said coyly.

"Shut up," Tony mimicked again.

He teased her all the way to the bus stop. They caught the city bus to Tony's house on Coplin Street and Kercheval, on the far east side of the city. There, Terri remembered meeting his mom, Verna, for the first time.

As Terri walked in the door behind Tony, Verna began to fuss at him.

"What took you so long getting home, Mane?" she began to inquire before she saw Terri follow in behind him. "Oh, never mind," Verna said with a look. "Okay, come in, gal," she said, excited to see who Tony had brought home.

"Mama, this is Terri," Tony said.

"Oh, you are pretty," she said warmly as she sized her up. "You the young gal that is always calling here?"

"Ha ha, Mama, cut it out," Tony said, looking a bit embarrassed.

"Yes, this is the gal that always interrupts my phone calls in the evening," Verna teased. "'Good evening, may I speak to Anthony?'" Verna said with a proper accent, mocking Terri.

Terri laughed a little uneasily.

"Well, come on in here. I made Mane's favorite," Verna said.

"Who's Mane?" Terri whispered to Tony.

"Ha, that's her nickname for me. It came from 'Little Man' when I was a baby, then she shortened to 'Man' as I got older, and then somehow became 'Mane.' Don't asked me how that happened. It must be our Mississippi roots," he joked.

That night they ate the best fried chicken wings Terri ever had with hot sauce, white bread, and red Faygo pop. Terri was in heaven. They must have eaten twenty wings.

After dinner, Tony walked Terri to the bus stop. He held her hand.

"So, what did you think?" he asked.

"Oh, those wings were the bomb," Terri said. "And your mom was really nice," she added.

"Yeah, I can tell she liked you," Tony said proudly.

"How do you know?"

"Because she never lets me bring girls to the house. She tells me to keep away from the 'chicken heads.' 'Don't be bringing any of them chicken heads to my house,' she always says," Tony explained.

"Do you have a lot of girlfriends?" Terri asked.

"No, just you."

Before Terri could respond, he kissed her on the lips.

Terri's strategy had prevailed—she had gotten the guy. Tony and Terri were officially an item. She would move in with Tony and Verna just a few months later.

4

Moms

"TONE, TONE! COME IN HERE!" TERRI yelled from the bathroom, her voice bubbling with glee.

Tony rushed in, slightly disheveled, as if he had just woken from a nap.

"What? Terri, are you hurt?" he asked, scrubbing the top of his head. He then saw Terri's wide eyes and even wider smile. She was holding a pregnancy test in her hand.

* * *

Two months prior, Terri had received a phone call from her mother. Their relationship was strained— seventeen-year-old Terri rarely heard from her mother, and when she did call, Terri usually let it go to voicemail. But this time, for some reason, she answered.

"Yes, Mother?"

"Peaches, your sister is pregnant," Calinda said. Her mother's joyous tone surprised Terri. On the rare occasion Terri would hear from her mother, she was typically antagonistic and condescending. Her sister Nikki was only nineteen, and the last time she heard from her she was sleeping on someone's couch. Pregnancy hardly seemed like something to be joyous about at this point. And Calinda was hardly ever happy when Nikki was concerned.

"Yes, can you believe it? I'm going to be a grandmother!" Calinda said.

Jealousy instantly washed over Terri. Even with the fractured, disappointing relationship Terri had with Calinda—that *Nikki* had with Calinda—both girls still sought love, attention, and approval from their mother. Terri wanted her mother to be that happy for *her*. And the sister rivalry was still alive and well. If Nikki had a baby, Terri wanted a baby.

After Terri ended the call with her mom, she laid down on the bed to reflect on her situation. Terri, a senior in high school, had finally found a place where she felt loved and cared for. Tony and his mother, Verna, had taken her in when no one else would—she felt like she had people who truly loved her. Being part of a family was important to her. But even with the safe, warm, caring place Tony and Verna provided for Terri, she was still lonely. So, so lonely.

She missed her brother. She missed her sister. She missed her mother and she longed to know her biological father. She wanted her family. And now that she heard her sister was having a baby and was starting her own family, Terri wanted that too. If Terri had a little girl of her own, she'd never be lonely again. And who better to have a baby with than Tony?

Tony and Terri discussed the possibility of having a child. She told him that he had to be like the mother, in the traditional sense. Terri's dysfunctional childhood left her lacking in the maternal instincts department, but Tony's love and compassion would surely make up for her. Besides, she wanted to be the breadwinner. Tony agreed.

"And I don't want to be a stereotype," she told Tony. "I don't want to be the single, Black baby Mama. I want to be your wife someday, so you can't cheat on me, Tony. I want us to have a happy family."

"I want that too, Terri," Tony said, then kissed her gently.

* * *

"So, what does the test say?" Tony asked.

"Tony, I'm pregnant!"

Terri couldn't wait to tell her mother.

* * *

"So, Mom, wait. You planned to have me? I thought you accidentally got pregnant," Zoe interrupted.

"Yes, that was a white lie I told you when you were younger because I didn't want you to think getting pregnant on purpose at seventeen was a good idea," Terri said as she searched her daughter's eyes for forgiveness. "I was young, I had lost my whole family, and I was searching for something. I thought I could find it by starting my own family. To have someone who would always love me," Terri explained as she wiped a tear from her cheek.

"Mom, please don't cry. I am not judging you," Zoe said.

"I know, love. I just feel bad I kept that from you all those years," Terri explained.

"Do you regret having me?" Zoe asked.

"Absolutely not, Honey!" Terri said to her daughter as she lifted her head and straightened her shoulders. "Do you remember when I told you that you were the best thing that ever happened to me?" Terri asked.

"Yeah, but most parents say that to kids to boost their self-esteem," Zoe said with a smirk.

Terri let out a little chuckle. "No, Honey. You *were* the best thing that happened to me. You forced me to focus. You forced me to work hard, to get going, to keep trying when times were really hard. I had to make it so you could have a better life than I did."

"Really, Mom?"

"Yes, Zoe. You are my saving grace. When I was younger and filled with anxiety and fear and I wanted to give up, the only thing that stopped me was you. Knowing you would not have a mom or a dad if I gave up. Knowing no one could take better care of you or prepare you for life the way I could. No matter how bad I screwed up. I wanted you to have the best life. And it's because of that love and care I pushed myself to be better professionally, yes, and a better person, too. I worked on myself. I worked on myself for you."

"Wow, that's deep, Mom."

"You were my savior, Zoe. Thank you."

Before Zoe could get in a word, Terri interrupted with a typical mom lecture. "Now you know that doesn't mean I condone having children out of wedlock, young lady."

"Oh my god, Mom. I know," Zoe said has she shook her head and covered her face with her hand.

"Listen, Sweetheart. I have zero regrets. Regrets are just wasted energy. What I will say if I would have had the knowledge I had now, I would have made a different choice then. I would have waited until after college, after I started my career and after I partied a little bit," Terri said as she chuckled.

"Oh my god, Mom," Zoe said, still shaking her head.

"I mean it, Zoe. Live your life to the fullest. Travel the world. Have adventures. Get your education, as much as you can. And once you have experienced life, choose to get married, and feel you are ready to dedicate your life to another human being, then have children. But not a moment sooner."

"Gosh, Mom. Finish the story."

Terri smiled. "Well, all right then."

5

I Have A Plan

TERRI WAS WORKING THE DAY SHIFT as a cashier at the corner drug store, Perry Pharmacy, and she had just gotten paid. Terri had just paged Tony's beeper to come pick up some diaper and formula money for Zoe, who was now four months old.

Terri was restacking the gum into tidy rows, waiting for Tony to pop in, when she saw *him* again—the third time this week. He waltzed into the store with purpose, wearing a dark blue suit and a leather messenger bag heavy with books. She didn't know his name—all she knew was that he was an incredibly handsome business school student not much older than she, who had been frequenting the store more often lately.

"Good evening, Theresa," he said in a deep, warm voice.

That was the first time she had heard him use her name. She didn't remember giving it to him. At first she looked puzzled, then looked down and, of course, saw her name tag on her smock, and blushed.

"I ... I wondered how you knew my name," she said. "Duh."

"You have such a beautiful smile," he said to Terri. She could feel her cheeks heating. She didn't know what to do with that comment. Terri looked down at her worn sandals, looked at the shelf of batteries she'd have to restock later, looked anywhere but directly at him. She felt so shy and so embarrassed.

The young man craned his neck to get into Terri's line of sight and said, "Theresa, my name is Roger. Roger Mason." He extended his hand to shake hers.

"Nice to meet you," Terri said, now grinning ear to ear. More confident in her smile, she let herself shake Roger's hand and really look at him.

He was a well-polished, immaculately groomed man. He had a chocolatey smooth face, a slick buzz cut, and perfectly white teeth that beautifully contrasted against his dark skin. He stood just over six feet, confident and full of promise. He was going to *be* someone. At eighteen, fresh out of high school with a four-month-old at home, Terri wasn't so sure she could measure up.

It didn't even cross Terri's mind that Roger was flirting with her. She was accustomed to talking to all sorts of strangers at her customer service job. And usually, the guys that flirted with her were boys from the neighbor-hood coming into the store to buy chips and pop. Roger always wanted something serious like pens or deodor-ant. One time he even bought foot pads for his shoes. This time he was looking for cologne. He asked Terri for a box of the Grey Flannel—the most expensive in the pharmacy.

"Fancy," Terri said under her breath.

"What was that?"

Terri looked up and said, "That's a fancy cologne. Not too many guys around here buy it."

Roger chuckled. "Not too sure how fancy it is buying cologne from the pharmacy." He let out a deep laugh and they both chuckled together. Terri wondered, though, why this struck him as so funny. She rang up the perfume and he paid with a credit card.

"Bye, Theresa," he said as he walked back out the front door, the bell tinkling behind him.

Roger returned to the store almost every evening shift Terri worked. They began to get to know each other. Terri started looking forward to seeing Roger when she worked, and was secretly disappointed on the rare occasion he did not stop in.

Then, late that summer, Roger came into the pharmacy with a bouquet of red roses clouded in tiny white buds of baby's breath. Terri figured he must be on his way out on a date and wondered about the type of girl Roger Mason liked.

She's probably a model, Terri thought. *She probably has an important job, wears nice dresses, and carries designer purses.*

But tonight, Roger didn't meander through the aisles looking for chocolate or perfume or whatever guys brought to dates. He walked directly to Terri at her cashier's post.

"Hi, Roger. What can I get for you tonight?"

"Nothing tonight, Theresa, I just saw these beautiful flowers and I immediately thought of you," he said so charmingly. "I thought you'd might like them."

Terri was in shock. She'd never had a guy buy her flowers before, except for one of her mom's many boyfriends when they were just trying to impress her.

Terri reached out to accept the flowers as she grinned. "Thank you, Roger. These are beautiful," she said.

"You are beautiful, Theresa," he said as he smiled his brilliant smile. But then, his smile faltered ever so slightly. He looked . . . vulnerable. Terri didn't know what to do with this moment. She said thank you one more time and that she had to go restock the tampons in the back. *Embarrassing.*

Terri moved swiftly through the aisles of the pharmacy and into the employee breakroom. She sat at the table and wondered what she was going to do with the flowers, what was she going to tell Tony? *Was* she going to tell Tony?

Terri's pager buzzed on her hip.

"411" flashed on the dull gray screen of her pager. She and Tony didn't bother putting in phone numbers for each other as they had their own private codes. 411 meant he was wondering what time Terri was coming home from work.

He had been up to see her at the pharmacy earlier that evening to pick up more money for diapers and groceries, but he was anxious for Terri to get home so they could hang out. They hardly did these days. Terri always got home just before Tony had to bolt off to his night shift at the gas station. Tony pumped gas from midnight to 7:00 a.m. while he was putting himself through junior college.

Terri didn't bother calling back. It was already 8:00 p.m., the end of her shift. She took off her blue work smock and headed for the breakroom. She grabbed her purse from the locker and paused, contemplating whether to take the flowers home. She pulled a tall plastic cup out of a cabinet and filled it halfway with water, then delicately arranged the roses. A small piece of paper fell from one of the petals, and she saw a phone number written in slim and loopy script.

Nothing actually happened, she thought. But Tony likely would wonder and wondering often led to jealousy. She didn't want to disrupt the flow of life they were operating within. She was already exhausted. No, she'd leave the flowers here.

She leaned over to smell them once more and left them on the breakroom table. She could see and smell them again tomorrow when she came in for her afternoon shift. She tucked the note in her locker beneath an old pair of socks and began her walk home.

As Terri walked home, she couldn't stop thinking about Roger. How with each interaction, he made her feel so beautiful and so interesting. He'd asked her about her plans for college. Terri had almost forgotten about those dreams. Under the weight of all the dysfunction, trauma, and confusion of her early teen years, somehow her dreams had gotten buried. But when Terri met Roger, she started digging deep into her spirit and heart to find her buried treasure.

But despite all that, she couldn't help feeling there was so much more to her; there was so much more life she wanted to live. She remembered asking her mom once if she had money for college. When her mom said no, Terri decided there was no reason to stick around. She would have a better chance out in the world on her own, so she'd ran away from home.

But four years later, she was no better off. She was eighteen with a baby, splitting her workdays between Perry's and Kentucky Fried Chicken. This was not what Terri had planned for herself. And her conversations with Roger reminded her of that. A tear slid down her cheek as she approached the little house she shared with Zoe, Tony, and Verna. She quickly wiped it away.

She could smell dinner even before she walked in the door of the two-family flat. She'd forgotten it was Tony's payday—Verna was frying the chicken Tony had picked up from the grocery store that day. Fried chicken wings with Frank's hot sauce were Tony and Terri's favorite. Verna would fry up a whole twelve-pack of wings, then they'd all sit in the backroom and throw down on them with red Faygo pop.

As Terri climbed the steps, she could hear Tony's anxious footsteps coming to the door to let her in. As he opened the door, she could see his wide smile. "Where you been? Mama is making fried chicken," he said excitedly.

"I know. I could smell them down the street," she said teasingly. "Is Zoe asleep already?"

"Yes, she is in Mama's room," Tony said, nodding to the door behind where her daughter slept. Terri quietly tiptoed into the room and saw her sweet baby sleeping so peacefully on her back. She was a true beauty. With caramel skin and dark chocolate ear lobes, she looked more and more like her dad every day. Verna said that eventually Zoe's whole body would be the color of her ears. Terri loved her multi-colored baby girl. As she stood there and watched her sleep, she kept thinking back to Roger. She thought back to her dreams, her future.

As she and Tony sat in the back room, chomping on a wing hot out of the grease, Terri was quiet, lost in thought.

"What's on your mind, T?"

Without thinking, Terri just blurted it out. "I want more to life Tony. I want a career."

Tony chuckled, "I know, T. I know you want more. We just got to figure it out," he said patiently.

"Well, I think I have a plan," Terri said hopefully.

"I know you do," he said and laughed. "Let's hear it."

"Okay, what if I went to the military while you finished college? And then when you finish college, I could use the money from the Navy to go to college, and then you could work to support us."

"Why would you choose the military?" Tony asked.

"My mom went to the Air Force and she liked it. It gave her opportunities," Terri said. "If I join, we could move out of here and have our own house on the base, just me, you, and Zoe."

"How long would that take for us to move?" Tony asked.

"I'm not sure, but I can go see the recruiter on my next day off. I do know we should definitely get married, too," she said. She bit into her chicken but glanced at Tony from the corner of her eye, trying to catch the expression on his face.

"Okay," he said without any hesitation.

Terri grinned her big Terri smile.

"Okay? Okay?" They both were smiling now, clutching each other's hands. Roger wasn't even a passing thought now. "We're getting married!" Both Tony and Terri laughed and grinned, and continued to eat their chicken and started making plans for the future.

* * *

Zoe began to chuckle. "I love Granny's chicken wings," she said, referring to Verna.

"I know, right?" Terri agreed. "With Frank's RedHot sauce," she said licking her lips.

"We should buy a couple packs and take them over to her house. See if she'll fry some up on Sunday?" Terri inquired with a sly grin.

"Mom, why didn't you ever fry chicken wings if you love them so much?" Zoe asked.

"Yeah, I was not much of a fried food person. I tried to cook healthy meals for you. I figured if we wanted fried chicken we could go to your Granny's or run out to Popeye's," Terri said.

There was a pause as they munched away at their lunch.

"So, did you have an affair with Roger back when you were with Dad?" Zoe asked with a devilish grin. "Playa Playa."

"Hey, I ain't a player, I just crush a lot," Terri said quoting Big Pun's hip-hop jam.

"Oh my god, Mom, you are so corny!" Zoe said laughing and snorting over her grilled cheese.

"Girl, you know I am hip," Terri said in between chuckles. "Don't hate the player, hate the game," Terri added as she burst into a deeper laugh.

"Mom, please stop. I'm begging you," Zoe said, seemingly, half-embarrassed, half-proud of having a mother that was easy to joke around with.

"No, but seriously, Zoe. I would never be unfaithful to your father or anyone for that matter," said Terri, growing serious again. "I had to tell Roger goodbye."

6

Goodbye, Roger

IT HAD BEEN ABOUT THREE MONTHS since Terri last saw Roger at the pharmacy. It had been that day he'd brought her the bouquet of roses with baby's breath and a note on fancy cardstock paper with his phone number. Since then, she and Tony had picked out a small diamond engagement ring. It wasn't much, but Terri thought it was beautiful. They'd gotten married at the local courthouse, with just Big Jimmy, Tony's brother, as their witness.

Tony shared everything with her—his mom, his family, and whatever little money he did make. He loved and looked out for her, and Terri loved him for that. Which is why, no matter how tempting, no matter how charming Terri found Roger, she was loyal to Tony. Terri knew she couldn't call Roger after her conversation with Tony about getting married, so Terri threw Roger's note along with the flowers in the breakroom trash can. She pictured Roger at his fancy house, waiting next to a phone that wouldn't ring. When she didn't call, he probably would know she wasn't interested. Roger hadn't returned to the store again, and Terri had put him out of her mind.

Terri was working at the electronics counter one day. As she was turned facing the back wall, restocking the batteries, she heard a deep voice.

"Excuse me, Theresa, may I have some help, please?" Terri was startled. No one called her Theresa. Well, except for Roger.

Terri turned around quickly with her big Terri smile.

"Hi, Roger!" she said excitedly. Roger was a bit thrown off guard by Terri's excitement. He had not heard from her. But he welcomed her enthusiasm and returned her energy with his gorgeous smile.

"It's been a while," Roger said.

"I figured you had pretty much bought up everything in the store," Terri chided.

Roger blushed, but then his facial expression became suddenly serious. The corners of his lips turned down. He looked at Terri's hand and saw a small diamond ring and a gold wedding band. Terri's eyes followed his. As she nervously fidgeted with her wedding ring, she tried to stay upbeat.

"Oh, yes, Tony and I got married last week."

"Wow," Roger said a heavy sigh. Terri could see the

disappointment on his face. In that moment, Roger stood frozen, as if to fight back tears.

Roger regained his composure, forced a smile, and said, "Congratulations, Terri. You are such a wonderful woman and you deserve happiness."

Terri's heart ached at that moment. It was as if time had stood still, and it was just her and Roger. Their eyes were locked on each other. Their eyes were talking to each other.

She hoped her eyes said, "I'm sorry. I wish it could have been you. I wish I would have met you sooner."

"Goodbye, Terri," he whispered, his eyes downcast.

He reached in his pocket and pulled out his business card and laid it on the counter. "If you and Tony ever need anything—anything at all—give me a call." Terri was speechless, breathless, and trembling all over as she watched Roger walk out of her life.

7

Breakin' My Heart

TERRI DIDN'T THINK SHE WOULD USE the card he'd left her when they'd said goodbye at the pharmacy. She had felt a sort of heartbreak for a love and a life that could have been—calling would have been too painful. But something inside her compelled her to keep it tucked in the corner of her locker.

A week later, in a moment of sheer panic, she had pulled it out and called him.

"This is Roger," Roger said in a serious, business-like tone. Terri could tell with just this greeting that he was on track to become a successful businessman. It was enough to break her heart all over again.

"Roger, this is . . . um—" Terri's voice cracked.

"Theresa?" Roger asked. "Theresa, it that you?"

Terri let a sob escape.

"What's wrong Theresa? Where are you? Are you safe?" Roger's voice strained with dire concern.

Terri couldn't speak, she just let the tears flow.

"Okay, Theresa, I need something from you, baby girl. Theresa, are you listening to me?" Roger asked with a sweet, yet commanding voice.

Terri took a deep breath, bracing herself for the pain that would inevitably come by uttering these words. "Roger, Tony went to jail!"

"Theresa, where are you, baby girl?" he said, his voice steady.

"You can't come here," she whispered.

"You're at Tony's house?"

Terri nodded, then realized of course he couldn't see her. "Yeah," she whimpered.

"Theresa, you and Tony live down the street from the pharmacy, correct?"

"Yeah."

"Terri, can you do something for me?" Roger gently coached Terri.

"Yeah."

"Theresa, I need you to walk to the pharmacy. I need you to wait for me there. I'll be there in less than ten minutes," Roger directed. "Terri, are you okay to walk to the pharmacy?"

"I don't want my boss to see me like this," Terri said, embarrassed. "I don't want you to see me like this either, Roger."

"Theresa, this is what I need you to do for me, baby girl. I need you to go in the house, grab your jacket and purse. Is Zoe with her grandmother now?"

"Yeah."

"I'll call you when I am down the street. I'm in a blue Jetta. I'll roll the window down so you can see that it is me." Roger paused. "Theresa, baby girl, be sure you know it is me. Okay, sweetheart?"

"Okay, Roger."

Terri stumbled four blocks down the road, past her friend Pearl's house where she and Tony used to hangout. Tony was friends with her brother Rob. Terri wondered if Pearl and Rob already knew. Terri wondered if her and Tony would ever get to hang out together again. So many thoughts were crashing in on her. The short walk to the pharmacy felt like an eternity.

Roger pulled up in his blue Jetta exactly where he told her to meet him and rolled down the window. His brows were knit together in concern. Terri stumbled her way into the car. When she reached the passenger side door, she let her limp body fall onto Roger's lap. She wept with uncontrollable sorrow.

Roger sat with the car parked. He rubbed Terri's back gently. He turned up the heat to keep her warm and turned up the radio to comfort her. "Breakin' My Heart" by Mint Condition played through the speakers.

Don't tell your friends
That I don't mean nothing to ya
Please don't deny the truth (pretty brown eyes)
Quit breaking my heart . . .

* * *

"Wow, Mom, you move fast!" Zoe quipped.

"Whatever, don't judge me," Terri teased back. It was what Zoe always said when her mom would comment on her life. Now the tables were turned. Zoe was an observer of her mom's early life.

"So, Mom, when did you and Roger reunite?" Zoe asked, remembering Roger to be an important person in her own life. Roger treated Zoe like his own daughter.

"Oh yes, this is the funny part," Terri said as she thought back to the time she reunited with Roger.

8

Cuban Sandwich

THREE YEARS LATER, TWENTY-ONE YEARS OLD, and with a few community college–level classes under her belt, Terri had now transferred to a four-year university. During her active tour of duty with the Navy, she'd decided to take a few college courses to use toward her bachelor's degree. Her goal was twofold. She had decided to take some of the harder classes, like math and economics, to get them out of the way before she transferred to a four-year university; one of her colleagues in the Navy suggested that to her. She also wanted to take the required courses for her freshman year and enter university as a second semester sophomore. Since she had taken a detour to the Navy first, she knew she'd be a bit older than the average freshman. She wanted to graduate from undergraduate as quickly as possible.

The G.I. Bill helped her and other people who served in the military pay for a four-year university. Terri had applied to several colleges, including the University of Connecticut, where she was stationed; Howard University in Washington, D.C.; Spelman College in Atlanta, Georgia; University of Detroit Mercy; and the University of Michigan-Ann Arbor. Terri had been accepted to all five colleges, but her heart was set on attending Spelman or Howard—historically Black colleges and universities, known as HBCUs. Terri didn't know much about HBCUs, but a friend of hers from the Navy said they actively embraced diversity and promoted empowerment of Black students. Terri didn't really know what that meant but decided to take her friend's advice and apply. She was thrilled when she was accepted to both, but reality was a rude awakening. If she moved to D.C. or Atlanta, she would not have the support network to help her raise Zoe.

Terri had applied to University of Michigan, largely because of Roger. He had been attending law school at Michigan when she had met him.

She hadn't seen him in years, but she always kept him close to her heart. Plus, she remembered Roger going on and on about their business school when he used to flirt with her at the pharmacy—how it was the very best around. And if she went to Michigan, she'd still have Tony's mother's support with Zoe. Zoe's paternal grandmother, Verna, was a true blessing. She looked after Zoe while Terri was in boot camp. Terri tried to bring Zoe to her Connecticut deployment, but it was difficult finding someone to help her babysit Zoe there. So, Verna stepped up again.

But Terri missed her daughter desperately during her deployment. University of Michigan helped their students with housing and childcare, so she could be near Zoe once more. All signs had pointed to University of Michigan, and so there she decided to go.

When Terri first arrived on campus, she had strolled through the historic halls of Michigan Union on the Ann Arbor campus secretly hoping she'd run into Roger. He would have graduated by now, but just the thought gave her butterflies. What would she say if she did run into him? Roger had captured Terri's heart even though they only had a brief time together prior to her leaving for the military.

The third time Roger had visited Terri at the pharmacy, he had gifted Terri a copy of a book called *Why Should White Guys Have All the Fun?: How Reginald Lewis Created a Billion-Dollar Business Empire*. It was about a Black businessman who facilitated the first international leverage buyout. Roger told Terri he wanted to be just like Reginald Lewis. He wanted to be a corporate mergers and acquisitions attorney. He wanted to buy, fix up, and sell businesses. Terri was so impressed and inspired by Roger's ambition. It helped her remember her own dreams she once had for herself. Terri had wanted to become a doctor, a surgeon—but all those dreams grew small when she had Zoe.

Both Terri and Roger spent a majority of their early

childhood growing up in poverty, but both their parents stressed the value of education. Roger's mother, Ann, was a single mother living on welfare, working as a waitress at a restaurant until she met Roger's stepfather, Aaron. Aaron Mason was an accountant by trade and was a managing partner of one the largest global auditing firms, PricewaterhouseCoopers. His job was to sell the firm's services to large corporate clients, and Aaron was a genius in his field. He sold multi-million contracts and on an annual basis, making the company about $200 million in revenue per year. He was one of fifteen managing partners, and the only Black man.

Aaron met Ann while she was waitressing at the new restaurant close to his office. He told Roger the story over and over of how he would go to the restaurant for lunch almost every day for a year until Ann agreed to go out with him. Ann was hesitant because Aaron always showed up with a finely dressed, beautiful, smart-looking businesswoman, who Ann later found out was the only other African-American managing partner in the auditing firm, who was happily married with three small children.

Once she learned that, Ann finally gave in to Aaron's coffee request. They were married a year later when Roger was a teenager. Roger admired Aaron for being a dad to him and a good husband to his mom. Roger's real father left when he was just an infant; he didn't remember him at all. But Roger felt fortunate he and his mom had Aaron.

Aaron helped Roger dream big. Aaron even used to take

Roger to his auditing firm. He let Roger sit in on meetings and took him to some of his client sites. Aaron was able to offer his son summer internships, which exposed him to a whole new world. Roger saw men in suits with briefcases, walking fast and talking on cell phones—these were *real* bosses. He saw women running meetings in high heels, elegant skirt suits, hair styled fashionably, and nails neatly manicured. Roger called these women "Boss Ladies." Roger knew he wanted to be a part of this world.

* * *

Terri was short of breath as she moved swiftly across campus to grab a bite in the short window of time she had. She'd just finished her Race & Ethnicity class with Dr. Tyrone Forman and, if she hurried, she could stop in Zingerman's Deli and grab a sandwich before her 3:00 p.m. shift started at the hotel. Terri was working a full-time job at the Hampton Inn five nights a week, waitressing at Max & Erma's on the weekends, and carrying a full-time course load of forty credit hours per year. With Tony in jail, Terri was a single parent living in campus family housing trying her best to juggle. The vast majority of her money went towards tuition, rent, and Zoe's education, and what was left she was saving for a new car. She was driving a used, 1987 red Dodge Shadow, now on its last leg. She knew she needed a more reliable car to get back and forth to work and to get Zoe to school, gymnastics—wherever else she needed to go. But this month, she had pulled together ten extra dollars to treat herself to a Zingerman's Cuban sandwich. She had been looking forward to this lunch all week.

She rushed up to the counter hungry and a bit disheveled. She ordered her sandwich, a Cuban with pulled pork, peppered ham, Swiss, dill pickle slices, and hot mustard on fresh bread. She had only had it twice before, but it was quickly becoming her all-time favorite sandwich.

Terri approached the cashier at the deli counter to pay and realized she had lost her only ten dollars. Her cheeks burned red and little beads of sweat began to form on her forehead. There was a line forming behind her. Finally, after she gave up searching through her backpack and as she went to apologize to the cashier, she heard a very gentle voice behind her in line.

"Please, put her sandwich on my tab."

Still shuffling through her overstuffed backpack in hopes that this ten-dollar bill would somehow materialize, she answered the gentleman without looking up. "Oh, no that's not necessary. I guess it wasn't meant to be."

This gentle stranger put his hand gently on her shoulder, which thoroughly took her by surprise.

"Please, it's my pleasure, Theresa."

That made Terri practically jump out of her skin. She *knew* that voice. "Roger?" Terri blinked in disbelief. Her heart raced with excitement.

"Hello, Theresa," Roger said with his signature, irresistible grin.

9

Perfect Date

AFTER RUNNING INTO ROGER AT THE deli, he'd walked her across the Diag to her Environmental Justice class in the School of Natural Resources. The Diag, which is a large, magnificent green space in the middle of Central campus, was super crowded that day, per the usual. There was an outdoor protest happening on one side and a student group hosted a fundraiser on the other. The activities on the Diag were very eclectic and always exciting. Roger used the congestion of the crowds as an excuse to hold Terri's hand, guiding her as they walked and talked.

Roger had been on campus speaking to a class of graduating law students, trying to recruit them to his firm. He was now an up-and-coming mergers and acquisitions attorney, just like he told Terri he would be. As a mergers and acquisitions attorney, he was responsible for making sure all the laws were followed when one company was bought out by another and merged into one company. These attorneys need to be super intelligent and knowledgeable about federal and state law, employment laws, and all aspects of corporate law. When she reached the School of Natural Resources, Roger had surprised her. He'd asked if she'd like to continue their conversation over dinner Friday. Terri had blushed and stammered on about tentative plans she'd have to cancel, but Roger persisted— and, of course, Terri agreed.

Terri had no idea what to wear to the dinner. She had to look *perfect* for her date with Roger. She knew with all the financial constraints she had, she could not afford to buy anything full price, so, in between her other jobs, she filled in a shift or two at various stores in Briarwood Mall to get employee discounts on shoes and clothes. This evening, Terri had finally settled on a sleeveless denim dress that she had purchased on employee discount from J.Crew and a pair of black strappy wedged heels from The Limited, also with her employee discount. She topped off her look with a swipe of powder pink lipstick. The outfit was, indeed, *perfect*.

She hadn't seen Roger in over three years, since the week they'd spent together after Tony was incarcerated—since the time he had been her knight and shining armor. In the three years since, she'd turned into a lady who could stand on her own two feet. She was not the little timid teenager who needed to be rescued. She had gained confidence in the Navy. She'd gained wisdom, and most importantly, she gained independence. She was a mother who worked hard to put her daughter through private schools all while studying herself. And she was not a victim of her circumstances—she was a *victor* over her circumstances.

Roger had asked Terri to meet him at a restaurant in downtown Detroit called the Rattlesnake, right on the riverfront and fancier than any restaurant Terri had ever set foot in. Terri smoothed her dress in the mirror and wondered if her outfit was appropriate. Looking at the white tablecloths and waiters in vests, she wasn't as sure anymore.

The hostess led Terri to a table in the back corner of the restaurant, where Roger stood waiting. He was looking at her differently than he did when he'd visited her at the pharmacy. As Terri walked toward the table, she watched Roger's gaze—he didn't take his eyes off her.

"Wow. Terri, you look beautiful tonight."

Terri blushed. "Thank you," she said, now thoroughly satisfied with her outfit choice.

Roger pulled out a chair next to the one he had his suit coat draped over.

The waiter came over with a bottle of expensive red wine and showed the label to Roger. Roger nodded and the waiter poured a splash of wine in his glass. Roger held the glass out to Terri.

"I want you to taste this wine and tell me what you think," he said. Terri had never had wine before, yet now Roger was asking her opinion. How was she to know if the wine was *good*? She took a sip, swishing the drink around her mouth.

"It's okay," she said, stifling a bit of a nervous giggle. She never really liked to show her vulnerability or inexperience. But Roger knew.

"First, Theresa, gently grab the stem of the wine glass and give the wine a gentle swirl to open up the bouquet," he gently instructed, touching her bronzed arm. "The bouquet is the aroma."

Terri let the scent of the wine waft to her nose as she swirled the glass. It smelled like . . . well, red wine.

"Next take a small sip, hold it in your mouth for a few seconds to let the flavor dance around on your tongue. And then swallow." Terri didn't know if Roger was being intentionally flirty or what, but her heart was racing, and her cheeks were almost as red as the wine. She did as he instructed.

"Wow, this is amazing, Roger!" she said, now with the adequate knowledge to tell. And it was. Roger nodded to the waiter, who proceeded to fill both their glasses.

Their first dinner together, after three years of being separated by silence, unknowing, and wonder, was magical. They laughed and talked for hours. The meal was decadent. Terri ordered filet mignon upon Roger's insistence that the cost was not an issue. The meat seemed to melt on her tongue.

As they talked and laughed, Terri felt herself falling in love with Roger again. And Roger let Terri see he was in love with her with the flutter of his eyelashes and the smile he couldn't keep off his face.

After they finished dessert and a spat of playful banter, Roger's face turned a bit solemn. He locked eyes with Terri, gently reached out, and took her hand in his. He leaned over a few inches from Terri's ear and asked, "Theresa, why did you leave without saying goodbye?"

Terri's heart sank.

"I don't want to bring up too much of the past, but I have to know why you just disappeared on me," Roger said, his eyes cast down.

Roger continued to fumble, something he hardly ever did. "I mean, we don't have to talk about this, Theresa. I mean if you don't want to ..."

Terri watched Roger struggle to find the right words. She could see the same love in his eyes now, sitting across the table from her, as the love when she disappeared three years ago. Honestly, she was relieved he broached the subject.

After Roger came to Terri's rescue that horrible night three years ago, Terri decided she would go on with her plan to join the military. She left a week later, without telling Roger goodbye. It took Terri a long time to forgive herself for that.

Terri reached over and caressed Roger's hand. "Roger, let me first tell you how sorry I am for leaving," Terri said as tears began to swell up in her eyes.

"Terri, please don't cry," Roger said, now clutching Terri's hand.

"No, it's okay, Roger. Crying helps me heal," she said. During her active duty service, the Navy offered free counseling and talk therapy as a support service to all the enlisted sailors. As soon as Terri arrived at her duty station in Groton, Connecticut, the first thing she did was look for a therapist. There she learned it was okay to cry as she confronted her childhood trauma.

But now, as a mother, sitting in front of Roger, she knew how important it was for her to let out some of the feelings she had inside. Her therapist, Vicki, had given her some tools she could use to cope with her emotions. Therapeutic crying was a tool to help her release some of the deep emotions she had, and she learned to be okay with letting out her feelings in safe spaces. And she knew she was safe with Roger.

10

Deep Dark

"**HOW MUCH OF YOUR PAST DID** you share with Roger?" Zoe asked.

"Over time I shared almost everything about my childhood, but not all at one time," Terri explained.

"My childhood experiences are very personal and very painful. I had to make sure I was strong enough to share without re-traumatizing myself. It took me years of therapy to arrive at a place of peace with my past. And not only peace, Zoe, but of acceptance that the challenges I faced created who I am today: a strong, compassionate, empathetic woman who fights for other children experiencing what I experienced or worse. My experiences motivate me to help heal the broken pieces of our communities of color. I learned trauma is intergenerational. I learned that the trauma my mother experienced plays a significant part in how she treated us as children. Anyway, I don't want to get preachy. But to answer your question, yes, I told Roger, and my sharing only made our bond stronger."

As Terri shared with Zoe, she remembered a particular time she had shared a deep hurt with Roger. It was a time he took her on a celebratory holiday to St. Bart's.

It was a surprise getaway after she graduated from the University of Michigan with her bachelor's degree in Political Science. Roger was so proud of Terri—she'd graduated at the top of her class, even while working full-time as a single mom, living in family housing on the university's campus.

Terri was proud of herself, too. She'd *earned* this vacation. And St. Bart's was just one of the many amazing places around the world Roger would be taking Terri. She leaned back into her cushy first-class seat on the airplane headed for paradise, feeling effervescent from the champagne and the pride.

Roger and Terri just lazed on the gorgeous white sand beaches for hours at a time. Terri loved how her skin would deepen with red and yellow undertones. Roger's would also darken and shimmer beneath the sun. And with their hands intertwined, the color contrast was so beautiful—yin and yang. Terri thought Roger was the most beautiful man she'd ever met. Not just because of his physical, finely sculpted, masculine qualities, but because of his heart. Especially his heart toward her.

Two days into their five-day stay, they were lazing in the warm, white sand, Terri's mood shifted inexplicably. Suddenly, she began to sob. Many times, over the previous years of Roger and Terri's relationship, Terri would fall into inexplicable depression, seemingly out of nowhere. Although these spells would only last for a day or so max, they were quite frequent, especially in the beginning of their relationship. Roger would pour into Terri, tell her that she was loved, show her a tremendous amount of compassion, grace, and emotional generosity. That helped Terri overcome the feelings eventually. Roger wanted to find more ways to help Terri, yet she wouldn't let him close enough.

They had been together now for almost four years—well, on and off. Terri had told Roger bits and pieces about her past—about Tony and Verna and Zoe—but no details beyond that, nothing that could crack open those wounds that still felt so fresh. Terri would often get angry at Roger and break up with him. Roger sometimes didn't call when he said he would when his schedule grew too hectic. In her mind, Terri created scenarios in which Roger was cheating, leaving her behind because she was too messed up to fit in his perfect world—and Terri had to break up with him before he could break up with her. Roger admitted that this was part of Terri he didn't particularly like, but he always stood by her. He wanted to love her. Every time she dumped him, he would give her a few days, and then find her. Both physically and spiritually he would find her, quiet her insecurities, and comfort her. Almost four years in, Terri knew Roger loved her, accepted her for who she was, and wanted to be there for her.

So on this particular day, with the St. Bart's sun heating her skin and college finally behind her, Terri was ready to share. She knew now she could trust Roger and that Roger would not judge her.

Terri began to open up.

"So, I told you my sister grew up in different girls' homes," Terri started.

"Yes, I remember you sharing that with me, Terri. I know that hurt you," said Roger.

"I can't help remembering the day it happened. I was downstairs, and I heard Nikki cry out. I ran upstairs to my sister's room and saw her nose bleeding. My mom and stepdad were standing on either side of her, and I asked what happened. My sister said Dad had punched her in the nose." Terri tried to blink back tears, but it was no use.

"I was so angry at Dad for hitting my sister, and so angry at Mom for letting him do it. I shouted at the top of my voice. I kept yelling uncontrollably." Terri had to stop talking for a second to catch her breath. Roger pulled her in close, wrapping his arms around her tightly as she continued to cry.

After several minutes, Terri looked up from Roger's comforting chest. "That's the day they kicked her out of the house," she said as she began to cry again.

"I remember looking at her outside my bedroom window. She was standing on the porch with a garbage bag filled with her belongings. I remember it so vividly. She was wearing these yellow capri pants and a white button-down shirt, holding a big green garbage bag. She was crying," Terri said underneath all the tears. "And her life has been really hard since then," Terri explained as she wept uncontrollably. She steadied herself slightly and continued. "But they never hit me, though, my parents. And I wonder if that's why my life is better than Nikki's. It's unfair—she was only fourteen.

"Before my sister was kicked out, growing up, I was like, ten, and my sister was twelve. My mom would fight my sister. I mean she would punch her with fists. One time I saw my mom punch Nikki right in the head. And I remember Nikki falling on this big green bean bag we had in the living room and my mom just jumped on her and began to choke her. I started yelling again, yelling at my mom, who was yelling at my sister. And me and my younger brother were just yelling at Mom, saying stop, Mom, please. Mom, stop."

Roger didn't say anything for a moment. Then he said, "Theresa, I am so sorry. I didn't know you had to go through all of that. Oh, baby, I am so sorry."

He pulled her in close to him and just held her as she wept.

"Why, why," she whispered.

Terri finally dosed off to sleep in Roger's lap and Roger fell asleep holding this beautiful, hurt spirit who he loved even more now hearing her story.

11

God

"HE REALLY LOVED YOU, MOM," SAID Zoe, her chin in her hands.

"Yes, he did. And I loved him deeply," she said.

"I can tell it was a different type of love than you had with Dad. I get what you are saying now. So what happened to Roger? One day he just disappeared. I can't remember what you said happened to you guys."

"Yes, I am getting to that, but first let me share with you one other aspect of Roger, an important one," Terri said as she remembered.

Terri was thinking back to when she first learned about God. *Really* learned about God. It was when Roger urged her to go to church . . .

Terri was twenty-six years old. She and Roger were

living in Chicago, Illinois. Terri was working for a top-tier management consulting firm and Roger was at a prestigious law firm. One Sunday morning, as Roger was tying a Windsor knot to complete his church look, Roger asked why she wouldn't come with him to the service. "What, do you think you will burn up or something?" Roger laughed.

Terri didn't think she would burn up, or at least she hoped she wouldn't ... she wasn't quite sure how all that worked. But her first introduction to God was a traumatic experience, which left Terri with little faith that God existed.

Terri remembered saying grace at the dinner table, but that didn't count. It always began with, "In the name of the Father, the Son and the Holy Spirit." Her stepfather would then say thanks for "these thy gifts which we are about to receive," which meant next to nothing to Terri. Terri thought her mother was brought up Catholic, where grace was something they practiced at every meal. However, her family never attended church, nor did they ever speak frankly about God, for that matter. But Terri did vividly recall a more in-depth look at religion when she was fifteen, after she had moved from Detroit to Grand Rapids to live with her aunt and uncle.

At her school in Detroit, there were bullies. Horrible bullies, who would beat and kick and scream at anyone who got in their way. Terri always tried to jump in and help whoever was getting bullied, so Terri then became a target.

One day as she was walking home from school with her friend Tina, Terri noticed a small middle school boy—the younger brother of one of her own bullies—picking on a bigger high school boy. The little boy smacked the larger boy in the head, spit on him, and talked about his mama. And the bigger boy didn't do anything. Terri couldn't stand injustice, even at a young age.

"Leave him alone," Terri said to the little boy as she made her way across the street. Tina urged her to mind her own business and to keep walking, but Terri was fearless in the face of unfairness.

As Terri drew closer to the little boy, all of a sudden, she felt a whack over her head, searing pain, and blood pouring down her face.

Before Terri could wipe the liquid from her eyes, she felt a foot kick her hard between her legs. Terri didn't know what was happening, but between blows from the bullies, she saw one tall, angry girl coming toward her with a fist clenched—the little boy's older sister. Terri took her umbrella that her mom had always made her carry in case it rained, and started whacking the hell out of the tall, angry girl. Terri grabbed a lock of her tangled hair with one hand and kept whacking her across the face with the umbrella from the other hand.

Terri yelled and yelled, not really realizing what she was doing—she just knew she had to defend herself. Suddenly, Terri found herself on the ground, being kicked in the head, the back, the stomach. The girls just kept kicking Terri and calling her names. After what seemed like forever, the kicking stopped. When Terri looked up, she saw the little boy standing over her.

"Next time, skank, maybe you will mind your own business," he said.

Terri let out a hopeless sob. She laid on the ground until she regained her composure. Tina helped her off the ground. Terri then turned to her friend.

"Did you see what was happening to me?" Terri said.

"Yes," Tina said, her eyes on her sneakers. "And that's why I told you to mind your own business," Tina said. They walked back to Mother Dear's house in silence.

When they got home and Mother Dear saw the bruises, she drew Terri a warm bath with Epsom salts and told her to soak for a while.

While Terri soaked in the bath, she had already decided she was not going back to that school anymore. She was too scared to walk down that street again. And she hated her school. Despite the metal detector, there was violence every day. As the salt stung her wounds, she remembered the one girl who was stabbed in her biology class with a pair of scissors. She just couldn't take it anymore.

That's when Terri decided to drop out of school and work full-time at Eastland Mall. There was no pressure, no fear, no fights. She didn't have to deal with the bullies on the walk to school nor did she have to deal with a tough environment there.

About six months into her new work routine, her Aunt Mary and Uncle John thought it would be best for Terri to come live with them in Grand Rapids and get back in school. There, Terri had a space for herself in a room in the basement. If you could even call it a room.

Terri would have rather stayed with her Aunt Jean and Uncle Bobby, who lived in Gross Pointe, Michigan, a suburb just east of Detroit—far away from her current school district. Terri and their daughter Crystal were the same age and used to hang out a lot, especially in the summers. Terri thought Crystal had the perfect life, with two parents who loved each other and loved their children. Crystal was allowed to go outside during the week, and she was allowed to hang out with boys. Terri and Crystal would always double date. If Crystal was dating a guy, Terri would be obliged to date his friend and vice versa. Most of the time Terri liked her match; but even when she didn't, she would play along so Crystal could have a good time. And Crystal exchanged the favor.

But Terri didn't get the chance to live with Crystal. Her Aunt Jean and Uncle Bobby had their own family to raise. Terri understood they couldn't take her into their home, but she really hated that she ended up with Mary and John in Grand Rapids. They were very much church-going people; they had two daughters and two sons, and they spent a few days each week at Bible study, church, and church func-tions. Living with them meant Terri was obliged to get into this practice. Although Terri had no idea who God was and really didn't understand the whole religion thing, she participated out of respect for tradition and rules of the home. This was her first real introduction to religion.

Terri lived with them for about eight months—long enough to get into an alternative school, which allowed her to catch up and get back into a mainstream high school. Terri always had book smarts; she was able to catch up quickly and resume high school and graduate on time at seventeen.

However, Terri didn't truly embrace God with her aunt and uncle. Terri guessed the reason was twofold: one, Terri really didn't understand God, and two, her aunt and uncle didn't have much credibility in her eyes. In church they were these nice, friendly folks, but at home they were something different. There was only anger and rage. Uncle John would have fights with his children—real fights with fists, shoves, and psychologically-damaging language. It was horrible; it was what Terri had run away from.

If God was present in that home, Terri didn't want anything to do with Him.

But God had been with Terri even before she knew He existed. Terri realized it was God's hand that had protected her when she ran away from home. He was there when she was bouncing place to place living with friends, running the streets. Although Terri never did or dealt, she was hanging out with drug dealers. They liked having her roll with them. She was cute and easygoing. And Terri liked rolling with them because she felt protected, she felt safe. Her friends had status in the streets, and Terri knew hanging with them meant survival.

At fourteen, what Terri didn't realize was the physical danger she put herself in. Riding in cars with guns and drugs; people were getting ganked all the time. She didn't understand the legal ramifications of appearing to be in possession of drugs and guns and how she could have destroyed life for her future self. She just knew she was accepted; she was safe, and she was cared for by this group of friends.

For whatever reason, Terri decided she'd go to church with Roger that Sunday. And when she stepped in church, all that past pain and misunderstanding flashed before her eyes and she realized she was also cared for by God. It wasn't her drug dealer friends that were protecting her when she was in the streets—it was God's hand the whole time.

* * *

"Zoe," said Terri, sipping the last of her sparkling water, "if there's one thing I want you to know, it's that God is with us all the time."

12

Dear Theresa

Dear Terri,

TERRI SAW THESE WORDS PRINTED IN Roger's thin, loopy handwriting on a beautiful pink lace envelope lying on the plush bed of their New York hotel. Terri had just arrived in the city—Roger had plans for them to catch *Les Misérables* on Broadway before dinner at one of New York City's finest French restaurants, *Le Bernardin*, the place Roger had proposed to her eight months ago. He had bent down on one knee to present her with the promise of marriage and a three-carat French-set Halo diamond engagement ring. Oh, how she loved that ring. Outside of Zoe, it was the most precious thing she had ever laid eyes on. As the picked up the pink slip of paper, she noticed it sparkle in the light.

Terri had graduated from the University of Michigan Ross Business School with her Master of Business Administration a few months earlier and was now just weeks away from starting a new job at a Big Five management consulting firm, Accenture. Terri was super excited. They offered her a starting salary of $110,000. Terri never imagined she would be making that type of money in her twenties. But thanks to one of her mentors who pushed her down the business path, she could now give Zoe a great education and send her to the best summer camps. And despite the fact she was engaged to Roger, who was making over $200,000 annually as a superstar mergers and acquisitions attorney, it was important to her to have her own career and make her own money. She wanted to be in a partnership with her soon-to-be husband as they began to build their dreams, their home, their business empire.

While they were in New York for this mini-holiday, she and Roger would be continuing their search for apartments in the city. Roger's responsibilities at his firm had increased, and he needed to be in New York at least once a week, so they thought it was smart and economical to just buy a small apartment in SoHo. Terri loved the idea—she always dreamt of having several homes around the globe.

This trip, Roger had come ahead of Terri for a few business meetings, and Terri was to meet him there Friday evening.

How sweet, she'd thought, when she spotted the little pink envelope. It must be another one of Roger's love notes.

She did find it odd that there was nothing else laid out on the bed. Anytime she and Roger would travel together, Roger would gift her an amazing dress for their first night on the town. But this time there was no box, no dress, no shoes. Just the pink envelope.

Terri gently picked up the envelope, which was a bit heavy. There was something more than just a letter inside. She grabbed a cold bottle of sparkling water and curled up comfortably on the sofa in the other room of the suite, eager and excited.

When Terri opened the envelope, she first saw the key. A smile immediately rose to her lips. Roger was surprising her with the apartment. He had come ahead of her to close the deal. And Terri knew exactly which one it was: a spacious three-bedroom flat she'd pointed out to him their last time there, the one with amazing lighting and a terrace Terri could use for her garden. The kitchen had all the upgraded amenities, including a rotisserie oven. Roger said it was a little too pricey not to be a main residence, but Terri begged playfully. Roger was not a cheap man, so if he said something was too pricey Terri knew to follow his advice. But she fell in love with that apartment.

As Terri began to picture her life in that apartment with Roger and Zoe, she started to cry. Her life was turning so beautiful like a storybook fairytale. She was overwhelmed with joy. As she wiped the tears from her eyes and wiped the little wet spots from the envelope, she pulled out a handwritten letter from Roger.

As she began to read the letter, her smile quickly faded.

I'm glad I was blessed with the opportunity to love someone as beautiful as you. From the first moment I walked into the pharmacy and saw your amazing smile and gentle eyes, you had my heart. I prayed every day to God that someday I would get the chance to love you. And when I finally did, our love was everything I imagined it to be and more. You changed my life, Theresa. You inspired me with your resilience and perseverance, you challenged me with your brilliant mind and strong sense of justice, you enlightened me with your enormous capacity to love and give of yourself to other, and most important, you loved me with your whole heart. You loved me the way I always imagined love could be, should be. Life with you was like a fairytale. The only difference is it was all real Theresa. Which is why it is breaking my heart to write you this letter ...

Tears blurred Terri's vision—she couldn't continue. Her hands began to tremble, and she began shaking her head as if to shake away the nightmare. She pulled the velvet throw over her and hugged the letter firmly against her heart and closed her eyes tightly, praying to wake up. But deep in her heart, she knew this was the last sound of Roger's heart she would ever, ever hear.

She received a call three months later from his mother. "Theresa, this is Ann."

Surprised and terrified, Terri answered. "Hi, Ann," Terri said.

"Theresa, Roger passed away this morning. He's finally out of pain." Roger had died of brain cancer. He didn't want to spend his last days having Terri watch him deteriorate. He spent them at a family vacation home in London, where his mom cared for him until the end.

* * *

Both Terri and Zoe had tears in their eyes as Terri finished sharing this story. Zoe loved Roger and just remembered the fun she had with him when she was a young girl. Zoe remembered how Roger made her mom smile. And Zoe also remembered when he wasn't around any longer.

"Mom, I'm so sorry. I had no idea," Zoe said as she reached over the table and caressed her mom's hand.

"Yeah, I never knew how to tell you Roger died," Terri tried to explain. "I just assumed . . ."

"Mom, I totally understand," Zoe said as she connected with her mother's watery eyes.

"Okay, thank you, Babe. Shall we go get ice cream now?" Terri said with a grin.

"Cold Stone?" inquired Zoe.

"Absolutely!"

Poem
You Love Me? How Can That Be?

You love me?

How can that be?

The runaway, throwaway, stowaway me?

You see me and you stay?

What is it that you see?

The hurt, the lost, the little Black me?

The me who cannot see my own beauty?

The me that feels everyone's pain?

The me that experiences everyone's rain?

You love me?

How can that be?

What is it that you see?

The depression

Confession

Obsession

Delusions

Confusion.

The isolation

Desolation

Desperation

Contemplation?

And after all that, you still love me?

How can that be?

You love me?

Part II

Please Don't Let This Happen To She

13

The Dang Ol' Dogs

A HARSH BUZZ ON WOOD JOLTED Terri from where she slept on the soft leather couch in her study.

The clock on the wall read 2:47 a.m. Before even looking at her phone, she knew within a five percent margin of error who it was. It had to be Omari. He was the only person who would call her at this hour, if she wasn't counting the one time Zoe called out of a sleepover when she was in fifth grade. This had to be her brother.

Still half-asleep, she grabbed her phone.

Messages:
Omari Erics

She contemplated not even opening the text. Depending on Omari's mood, the message could set her off into an emotional tailspin. Terri sighed and swiped open the text.

Sis you should call Dad and at least wish him Happy Holidays. He is alone by himself in that house. Come on Sis, do the right thing. I love you, Omari.

Terri's eyes rolled to the back of her head and she let out a long-winded sigh. She could not stand when Omari sent her these redundant, probably tipsy text messages every year around the holidays. He did this every year—trying in vain to patch together their broken family. Who was he to guilt her into calling their stepdad? That would only dredge up past trauma that Terri had spent years working to put behind her.

Omari and Terri's relationship had, however, strengthened over the years, especially since Omari had cut back on his drinking. He still lived in Austin, Texas, where Terri spent her most tumultuous adolescent years. Although he claims he graduated from the University of Texas, no one in the family was invited to the graduation or had set eyes on the degree. That was a running joke between Terri and her sister Nikki—one that always got Omari in a huff. Terri and Nikki loved their brother dearly, but they knew he could lie with the best of them.

In his early adult years, Omari struggled with drinking. Terri recalled one holiday season when Omari was visiting her and Zoe; unbeknownst to Terri, Omari was sneaking into Terri's gigantic quarter jar, then cashing the coins at the neighborhood party store for pints of vodka. Terri only realized after Omari left to go back home that her quarter jar was completely empty. There had to be over $100 worth of quarters missing.

Years later when Omari joined Alcoholics Anonymous, he felt a brotherhood with men who struggled just like him. AA helped him on his healing journey, and he was able to create enough stability in his life that he could hold down a job. Now Omari was a successful electrician with a small family-owned commercial and residential electric repair company in North Austin. Omari was still single. Because of the past he, Terri, and Nikki had shared, he too had trouble in the healthy relationship department. But when all else failed, he always knew he could rely on the love of his sisters in his darkest moments.

Nikki and Omari bonded in a different kind of way than he and Terri had. So, when tragedy struck Nikki three years prior, it permanently damaged a piece of Omari's heart. Nikki and Omari bore the brunt of their mother's sickness. Omari had it so bad that Child Protective Services had to take him out of their home when he was just ten years old. Omari had suffered from post-traumatic stress disorder all his life, and Nikki's tragedy almost took him over the edge. He made several half-hearted and unsuccessful attempts to take his own life.

As much as she loved her brother, dealing with Omari's emotional highs and lows could be exhausting, especially at 2:47 in the morning when she had a very important breakfast meeting in less than five hours. But she knew he was trying to do better. There was a time in Terri's journey that she made those type of 2:00 a.m. phone calls to Roger. And every time Roger picked up and every time he showed Terri compassion. Terri wanted to do the same for her brother. She was trying to be that person for Omari, like Roger had been that person for her. She propped herself up on her luxurious feather pillow and returned his call.

Her brother picked up on the very first ring. "Sisterrrrr!" Omari slurred.

"Hey, Omari," Terri responded, a tad annoyed her brother was a bit tipsy and awake so early in the morning. She took a breath, and let the annoyance go.

"Sister, I j-just sent you a text," Omari said with a slight stutter he'd had since he was a little boy. He had almost mastered his diction as a grown man, but when he became excited or inebriated, he still had a hard time controlling it.

Terri remembered their mother slapping Omari upside the head every time he stuttered. It was a horrible memory that still washed over Terri every time her brother's speech would slip. His stepdad used to follow Calinda's lead and physically or verbally penalize Omari for stuttering.

"Boy, what the hell is wrong with you, talking like that?" he'd say, slapping him on the back of his head.

These flashbacks previously flooded Terri's brain, over-whelming her emotions every time she talked to Omari. Tears would well in her eyes. However, she had come to a place on her healing journey where those memories were still present, but the negative emotions associated with the memory was no longer painful. Terri felt she had worked hard to arrive in a strong emotional space and was careful with Omari. Sometimes without knowing it, he would say something that could potentially trigger a memory. Omari lived in the past; he had not sought out the same type of emotional supports Terri had and, in many ways, was still grappling with his childhood on his own.

"Yes, I received your text. Omari, you drive me crazy trying to force a relationship that I have moved beyond," Terri said, rubbing sleep from her eyes.

"S-S-Sister," Omari stuttered. "You can at least give Dad a call. It's the holidays."

"Omari, K.C. is not my father. You can claim him as your dad if you want to, but I will not. Not after what he's done. And it's not fair that you try to force that on me," Terri said, feeling like a broken record.

"The past is the past. Besides, it was mostly Mom, and now that she is dead—"

Terri cut him off.

"No, Omari. It was not just Mom. When Mom was abusing you, he could have stepped up, spoke out about it, and got us all some help. But what did he do? Not only did he allow it, he followed in her footsteps. Do you not remember him beating you and Nikki and the dang ol' dogs?"

"Yes, I know—I do, but . . . but . . ."

Terri wondered for about the hundredth time why Omari would ever want a relationship with this man.

"But nothing, Omari," Terri interrupted. "I have forgiven K.C. as a part of my healing journey, but that doesn't mean I have forgotten. And for my own mental health I choose not to have a relationship with him."

"But Sister, what did he ever do to you? You were the favorite."

"The favorite, Omari?" Terri said, exacerbated.

"Terri, that's why you have the world knocked. And Sis, I am proud of you, but I'm just saying. You have a house, you are a doctor, you wrote books, you have lived abroad . . . Sis, your life is perfect. And it's perfect because Mom and Dad treated you like you were perfect," Omari said.

His words stung. Omari had no idea how much anxiety, pain, and guilt this sentiment had caused Terri over the years. Although now, Terri had learned, for the most part, to let these comments roll off and pass through her psyche without latching on and having a party in her brain. During her adolescent years and well into her womanhood, comments like these from her siblings paralyzed Terri.

Why had she escaped the wrath? Why did her mother and stepfather target their rage toward Nikki and Omari, sparing her? Why didn't she receive harsh punishments?

Terri had struggled with this internalized guilt for years. It was heartbreaking. It was joy limiting. It was sad. As a teenager and young adult, Terri felt she didn't deserve to be happy. Terri struggled with depression for years. The false guilt was a fog that followed her, a fog that did not allow her to enjoy many of the early successes she achieved.

She felt guilty celebrating important milestones like college graduations with her siblings. Terri was the first, and only, in her family to graduate from college, she had three advanced degrees, yet she was ashamed. So she never invited her siblings to the ceremonies. She didn't think they would be happy for her—Terri didn't think she deserved to be happy for herself. She knew her happiness would probably make them sad and even more resentful.

Even more devastating than feeling the shame of her own success was watching her brother's difficult personal journey unfold. He had so many struggles, so many disappointments, so many setbacks, so many poor choices that led him to a life of which he was not particularly proud. He had not been able to pull all the pieces together to achieve many of his dreams.

Terri felt similar guilt with her sister. But the guilt she felt with her sister was a different guilt, a deeper guilt.

Sitting on the phone with Omari now, she felt the guilt wash over her.

And she began to tell Omari stories of their childhood from her perspective. And he listened.

14

The Favorite

"**Peaches, what's wrong?**" Calinda asked her seven-year-old daughter. Little Terri had run to her bedroom and hid under the bed.

"Peaches, come from out from under the bed and let me talk to you," Calinda said softly.

Terri reluctantly crawled out from under her bed, big tears welling up in her eyes.

"What's wrong, baby?" Calinda asked.

"Nikki got presents and I didn't," Terri said, arms crossed and a bottom lip poking out.

"Peaches, it's your sister's birthday. You get presents on your birthday, don't you?"

The prolonged silence from her daughter and the sad look on her face broke Calinda's heart and prompted her to say, "Okay, would it make you happy if I gave you a present too?"

Terri looked up with her puppy dog eyes and pushed a smile through her pouting lips. "Yes, ma'am," she said.

Calinda reached over, pulled little Terri close, and kissed her forehead. "All right, Peaches," Calinda said with a sigh of easy defeat. Calinda's easy surrender, unbeknownst to her and little Terri, set a terrible precedent that created a life-long sibling rivalry.

Every year, Nikki had to share her birthday with her spoiled little sister. When Nikki received roller skates for her tenth birthday, Terri received roller skates for Nikki's tenth birthday. When Nikki was given a rabbit for her eleventh birthday, Terri received a rabbit for Nikki's eleventh birthday. This tradition had become so routine in their home, Nikki didn't bother to put up a rebellion. Plus, Terri secretly suspected Nikki liked her bratty little sister to have the same toys she had because they could play together. But Nikki never let Terri live that down; she teased Terri endlessly about being a spoiled little brat. And Terri never gave her sister a break either. She competed with Nikki for everything, even boys.

15

Grape Nerds

Gerald Foreman is so fine! He kissed me today before gym and asked me to meet him at the basketball game after school. And of course, I'm going to go!

TWELVE-YEAR-OLD TERRI WAS HIDING BENEATH THE large oak desk in her sister's bedroom, scraps of paper compiled in her lap. She brushed a wood shaving off the paper as she read Nikki's loopy handwriting. Her fourteen-year-old sister kept all her love letters and notes she passed in class in her hamster Brownie's cage. She'd hidden the notes underneath the newspaper linings that were covered with wood shavings to keep them out of Mom's sight, but also keep them dry from Brownie's pee and poop. When

Nikki was out, Terri loved the thrill of sneaking into her sister's room to play with Brownie and read her letters.

This letter was a back-and-forth letter between Nikki and one of her girlfriends discussing the hottest guy in the ninth grade. Gerald was the most popular boy at David Crockett High. And he was, indeed, so fine. Tall and lean, he had caramel brown skin and a light shadow of a mustache. He looked like a man already, but with a boyish grin that melted all the girls' hearts. And although he was known for being a player, girls flocked to him anyway. He was charming, charismatic, and incredibly cool.

And he liked Nikki.

Terri was still in middle school, but she saw Gerald all the time. He would visit his little brother in Terri's grade and play basketball with him at the middle school. Terri had been harboring a secret crush on Gerald as well, but she knew a freshman in high school would never consider liking a seventh grader. And the fact that Gerald had kissed her sister burned her insides a little.

A week later, Terri was allowed to stay after school for the middle school boys' basketball game. Nikki was on punishment for something that week and couldn't chaperone, but Bedichek Middle was only one block from their house, so Calinda was okay with Terri walking by herself to and from the game.

Terri had on a lime-green short set that day, one she thought she looked cute in. She rolled up the bottom of her shorts to show off her long-bowed legs. Boys always joked about her and said she walked like she rode a horse, kind of gap-legged like a cowboy. But her sister, Nikki, told her boys liked that; that's why they teased her. Nikki was always giving Terri tips about boys.

When Terri left the bleachers at halftime with her friend Kimi, she saw Gerald standing by the gym doors. Kimi and Terri giggled as they walked by Gerald, looking down, at each other—looking anywhere but directly at him.

As Terri passed by Gerald, he touched her elbow and said, "Hey, Terri."

Terri smiled her wide Terri smile.

"H-Hi, Gerald," she giggled. She couldn't believe he knew her name.

"What's up?" he said.

"Nothing, just here with my friend Kimi," Terri said sweetly. "Nikki is not here. She's on punishment," she felt the strange need to add.

"Aw yeah, that's right. Nikki is your sister," Gerald said, scrubbing his buzz cut with his hand. "Wonder what she did this time. Seems like she's always grounded!" he joked.

"Yeah, that's true," Terri said under her breath. She was a little ashamed because she knew it was a little deeper than just being grounded, but she wouldn't dare say that to Gerald. Terri knew the rule to never discuss family business in public. Calinda had a lot of rules.

"Hey, I'm going to walk to 7-Eleven to get a Slurpee and some chips. You guys want to come?" Gerald asked.

Terri looked at Kimi and giggled. "Sure!" Terri said.

They walked down across the track in the back of the school, heading toward 7-Eleven. Terri couldn't believe that Gerald Foreman wanted to buy *her* snacks at 7-Eleven! And Terri couldn't wait to get home and tell Nikki about it. This time, Nikki would be the jealous one.

When they entered the store, Gerald turned to Terri.

"Would you like something?" he asked.

"Yes, I would like some Nerds, please," Terri said shyly.

"Pick out the ones you like. And you can get something else. You can get Kimi some too," Gerald said. Cute *and* generous!

The three of them slowly walked back to the school. Chatting, giggling, enjoying their treats. Terri jumped on Gerald's back for a piggyback ride and Gerald raced down the sidewalk with Terri as his passenger. Terri screamed and laughed, hardly believing her luck. Gerald put her down, then jokingly tried to jump on Terri's back. Surprisingly enough, Terri was able to carry him a few feet before they both fell on the grass, limbs entangled. All three of them laughing with smiles stained blue from the blueberry Slurpee drinks and purple and pink Nerds.

When they finally arrived back at school, the basketball game was wrapping up.

"I need to find my brother," said Gerald. "But I had fun with you, Terri. We should hang out again."

"Aren't you hanging out with my sister?" Terri asked.

"Nah. I kissed her last week, but I like you now," Gerald said.

Terri blushed. She liked Gerald too, but couldn't believe he liked her over her sister. Nikki was beautiful; she was rehearsing to be a model. Why would Gerald choose her over a model?

"You kissed her?" She feigned ignorance.

"Yeah, but it was just a peck on the lips," he clarified.

"On the lips?" Terri exclaimed. "That sounds serious. You guys are boyfriend and girlfriend," Terri said jokingly.

"No, I didn't use any tongue," Gerald said. "Tongue kissing is for boyfriend and girlfriend."

Terri knew that was the rule. French kissing meant you were boyfriend and girlfriend, but she just wanted to hear if high school freshmen abided by the same code. Who knew? Maybe going to second base or booty squeezing was the threshold for commitment in senior high. She'd have to check her sister's notes later.

Kimi quietly observed their interaction, giggling the whole time. She finally said, "Okay, this is too much for me. I'm going back in the gym. Gerald, I'll tell your brother you're outside."

"Cool, thanks," Gerald said, grinning his irresistible grin.

Terri was a little more nervous now that her friend was gone.

"So, do you want to hang out again?" Gerald asked. "Maybe I can take you to Subway? Kimi can come with us. I think my brother likes her."

"Really? She thinks your brother is cute, too!" Terri shared, then clapped her hand over her mouth. She wasn't supposed to tell! But Gerald threw his head back and laughed. "We'll let them figure it out then," he said.

Suddenly, Gerald leaned down and kissed Terri on the lips. Gerald's lips were soft, and his breath tasted like grape-flavored Nerds. Terri liked it, but she felt a knot forming in her stomach. He was moving fast. *And Nikki liked him.*

Gerald pulled his lips away and put his forehead to Terri's. "Did you like my kiss?"

Terri's heart was beating so hard she could feel it in her ears.

"Um, yes," Terri said shyly.

"May I kiss you again?" Gerald asked.

Terri chuckled coyly and said, "Yes, you may."

Gerald gently grabbed Terri's chin and kissed her quickly. His tongue darted in and out of her mouth. Terri had no idea what to do. She just kept her mouth open and moved her tongue in circles. Her sister Nikki had once demonstrated this technique for Terri and Omari on one of their dolls. Nikki told them to always close their eyes—that made it romantic.

Terri kept her eyes closed and Gerald kissed for what felt like ages. She didn't know what to do with the saliva building up in her mouth. She didn't know whether to hold it in her mouth and spit it out at the end or just swallow it. She decided the latter would be more ladylike.

"So, now that means you are my girlfriend," Gerald said to Terri.

"Okay," Terri said.

It was late and Terri had to get home immediately after the game. She told Gerald goodbye as they made plans to meet at Subway the next day during lunch.

As Terri rushed through the door to her house, just in time to beat the curfew, she couldn't wait to tell Nikki.

Terri burst through the front door, startling Nikki, who was sitting on the couch reading and waiting for Terri to come and tell her about the game.

"Nikki, guess who asked me to be his girlfriend?" Terri said with overwhelming satisfaction and smugness.

"Who?"

"Gerald Foreman," said Terri, with all the syrupy spite she could muster.

There was silence for a moment as Nikki processed this information. Her face seemed confused at first, before her expression settled in rage.

Suddenly, Nikki was on top of Terri.

Terri screamed as her sister straddled her, pulling her braids and pinching her arms.

"Nikki, stop! I'm gonna tell Mom!" she shrieked.

"Oh, you want to go run to your mommy now, huh, Peaches? Are you planning to tell her you kissed a high school boy?" she said tauntingly as she pinched the soft skin near Terri's armpit hard. "You *knew* Gerald was my boyfriend," Nikki said with malice and hurt.

"He said he wasn't your boyfriend! He said you didn't even French kiss!"

"We did kiss," Nikki said.

"Well you didn't *French* kiss. He just pecked you on the lips," Terri rebutted.

"How do you know?"

"He told me!"

"So? He was still my boyfriend! And you *knew* that!"

"I didn't know! I promise," Terri lied.

"You did know, you ugly brat. How could you do that to me? You always just *have* to have what I have. You are a spoiled, stealing, lying, ugly brat!" Nikki said angrily to her sister.

"Get off me, you ugly duckling!" Terri screamed, trying to shove her sister off her. But Nikki was three inches taller, stronger, and had the upper hand.

"I can't help it if Gerald likes me better than you! I guess *I'm* the model," Terri teased.

Nikki pinched Terri even harder with one hand and yanked a braid with the other.

"Ow, ow!" Terri started to cry.

"I don't want to see those crocodile tears, you brat!" Nikki yelled. "You are no model, you fat ugly brat!"

Terri cried even harder. She could feel her skin start to tear from Nikki's fingernails, but her sister's words stung even worse than the welts. But in a way, she thought she deserved it.

"You're hurting me! And I'm not fat. Get off me, bully!"

"Peaches! Nikki!"

Both girls fell still and silent when they heard their stepfather call their names.

"Yes, sir?" they answered in sync, suddenly serious.

"What are you doing back there?" K.C. asked.

In unison once again they both answered, "Nothing!"

Even though Terri was getting pulverized by her big sister, she didn't want to even think about the punishment Nikki would receive if her stepdad knew she was beating her up. If he saw the welts on Terri's arms, he would terrorize Nikki. No matter how much Nikki hurt her, she did not want to see Nikki versus K.C. She was tired of how her stepdad punished Nikki. She hated it. She hated him much, much more than she hated her sister at the moment.

Nikki let go of her sister's braids. They locked eyes, and both sisters knew they had to call a truce. Terri and Nikki quickly moved away from each other, straightened their mangled clothes, smoothed their hair, and went to their respective corners without another word.

16

Cookie Burglars

TERRI HAD LOST RESPECT FOR K.C. long before she turned twelve. For all their sibling rivalry, she still hated the way he treated Nikki—and Omari. And she hated that he let her mom hurt them, too. If he was a real dad, he would have kept everyone safe. But instead, he was such a pushover. He did what Mom wanted and joined in on the abuse. And the abuse continued to escalate as they all got older.

They had lived in Austin for about four years now, and Terri couldn't figure out why the rage and terror had intensified in the house. Nikki and Omari were always under attack.

Terri remembered one time the abuse was particularly bad. Nikki had just come home from a basketball game when their stepfather asked Nikki if she was wearing makeup. She had tried to wipe it off before she had gotten home, but it was obvious. The smudges around Nikki's eyes and lips gave her away.

Nikki lied and told her stepfather no, she didn't have any on. He kept questioning her, waiting for her to break down and tell the truth. But Nikki was unflappable. When she made up a lie, she stuck to it. K.C. kept drilling her and drilling her until he grew tired of the verbal banter.

He grabbed Nikki by one arm and twisted it behind her back, shoving her into the interior wooden beam that separated the living room from the dining room.

"Ouch, you are hurting me!" Nikki screamed.

"I don't give a damn," K.C. said coldly. "You gonna tell me the truth?" he asked.

"I'm telling you the truth! Now get off me," Nikki screamed.

"Shut the hell up," K.C. said to the girl he called his daughter.

"Stop, you are going to break her arm!" Terri shouted from the corner.

"Go to your room," said K.C. His grip on Nikki remained firm.

"Stop, Dad! You are going to break her arm," Terri shouted again.

"Go to your room, young lady, right this moment!" K.C. warned.

"No!" Terri said defiantly.

Terri didn't respect K.C., but she wasn't scared of him either. She knew he wouldn't touch her. If he did, she would tell Mom, and then it would be K.C. in a world of trouble.

"Dad, stop. Or I am calling Mom," said Terri with all the courage she could muster.

"You better not bother your mother at work," K.C. spat back.

Nikki remained pressed against the beam, writhing to get loose. Tears streamed down her face, smudging the remnants of makeup even more. Her cheeks flushed red with pain.

Terri ran in the kitchen and picked up their house phone to call her mom, who was working the night shift at the IRS. Terri knew not to call her mom at work unless it was an emergency, but this was an emergency.

"Hi, Mommy," Terri said as Calinda picked up her extension.

"Hi, Peaches. What's wrong?" Calinda said immediately.

"Dad is twisting Nikki's arm. He is hurting her. He has her against the beam, and he won't stop twisting her arm. He is cursing at her!" Terri said frantically with her voice consistently escalating into a higher and higher pitched scream as she explained what was happening, unable to contain her emotions.

"Well, what did Nikki do?" she asked coolly.

* * *

"Nikki, are you asleep?" Terri whispered in the dark as she tiptoed to her sister's bed, hours after the fight.

Nikki stayed silent, and Terri watched her sister's chest rise and fall. It was about 1:32 a.m. Dad had twisted her arm badly earlier that day, and Terri wanted to make sure her sister was okay.

"Nikki?" Terri asked again as she gently shook her sister awake.

"Hey, Peaches," Nikki whispered, still groggy.

"Are you okay?" Terri asked as she sat down on the edge of Nikki's bed.

"I hate Dad," Nikki said, rubbing her eyes.

"I hate him, too. He is a bully," Terri said.

"And an asshole," Nikki said.

"Yeah, a big hairy asshole with hemorrhoids," Terri said. She looked at her sister with a half-smile, and they burst into muted laughter.

"Shhh," Nikki said, lightly hitting Terri on the shoulder. "You'll wake up the hairy asshole!" Terri and Nikki both knew what might happen if they did, indeed, wake their stepfather. That punched the joy out of them, and they fell silent again.

"Nikki, why did you lie about wearing makeup?" Terri asked.

"It didn't matter if I told the truth. Dad was just waiting to punish me," said Nikki. "Mom pushes Dad around—tells him what to do—and she doesn't even love him. And he knows it. So he takes his rage and anger out on us. On me."

"That's not fair. You are not supposed to beat your own children," Terri said matter-of-factly.

"Yes, I know, Peaches. That's why he is a big hairy asshole with hemorrhoids," Nikki said again, the ghost of a smile spreading across her face.

Nikki is resilient, thought Terri. She would get beat one moment, then joke about it in the next. Terri wondered how her sister could be so brave knowing that a punishment was always waiting around the corner for her. And not just any punishment. Brutal punishments. Like the one earlier. Twisted limbs, bruised ribs, bloodied noses— and then, of course, the butt whoopings with Dad's big black leather belt.

Terri had received just two butt whoopings in her life. Both from her stepdad and both when her mom was at work. And both times Calinda had been furious when she found out. Terri, unlike Nikki and Omari, was off-limits. But that still didn't stop Terri from getting into mischief— although not as bold as Nikki, she was clever and sneaky.

"Hey," said Nikki. "How about we go sneak some of those double chocolate chip cookies Mom made earlier?"

As a rule, in Calinda's house, once the children were in bed for the night, they were not allowed to get up except to go to the restroom. Terri was already breaking the rules being in Nikki's bedroom.

Tonight, they would have to be strategic.

If they were not careful, they'd be caught. But if they pulled this off, Calinda would assume K.C. was to blame for the missing cookie. He had a serious weakness for them. Terri and Nikki snuck down the stairs, careful not to step on the squeaky one. Tiptoeing through the living room, both girls made their way to the kitchen. Calinda kept the cookies out of reach on top of the refrigerator. They quietly lifted the barstool from the dining room and quietly carried it into the kitchen. Nikki held the stool still while Terri grabbed one cookie.

The girls split the cookie in half and quickly gobbled their shares. Calinda made the *best* cookies.

"We should get another one," Terri suggested.

"Peaches, you are so greedy," Nikki laughed, and Terri laughed with her.

"I know," Terri laughed. "Want to?"

"Yes, but let me do it. I'll arrange the cookies to look as if none are missing," said Nikki.

"Okay," Terri said.

Nikki gracefully clambered atop the barstool to reach the jar. She stood there for longer than it would realistically take to simply sneak a cookie from the jar.

"Nikki, what are you doing?" Terri whispered.

"Nofin, Peashes," she said, her mouth full of cookie. Nikki was stuffing her face with more than her share. Terri started shaking the barstool.

"Share Nikki, you have to share!" Terri whispered too loudly and began shaking the stool.

Nikki began to giggle and let out a little squeal. Suddenly, they heard movement around upstairs. It was

K.C. He must have heard them. Nikki rushed to close the cookie container and quickly climbed down off the stool.

"Hurry, hurry," Nikki whispered frantically.

Both culprits clumsily scurried across the kitchen floor into the dining room, replacing the stool. They started running down the hall when Nikki realized she still had a cookie in her hand.

"Oh no," she whispered.

A mischievous smirk rose on Nikki's lips. She balled the cookie in her fist and started walking toward their brother's room.

"Where are you going? Dad is coming!" Terri warned her sister.

"I'm putting this cookie in Omari's room so if Mom and Dad see some missing, they will think it was him," said Nikki.

"Oh, good idea," Terri said, though a twinge of guilt rolled in her stomach.

The cookie burglars tiptoed into Omari's room, careful enough not to wake him but swift enough to avoid getting caught. Terri gently lifted Omari's pillow and placed the cookies under his head.

They both snuck into Terri's room, which was closest to the kitchen and pretended like they were asleep just in time.

K.C. appeared in the doorway. "Nikki, what are you doing downstairs?" he growled.

"Terri was scared because she heard a noise, so I was comforting her," Nikki lied.

"A noise?" K.C. asked.

"Yes, but we think it was Omari. We saw him sneaking cookies from the kitchen," said Terri.

K.C. turned on his heels quickly, a sharp military turn. He marched swiftly to Omari's bedroom. He hit the light switch so hard, Terri could see the light flicker on and back off again.

"Omari, boy I know you are not asleep. Get your butt out of bed!"

Nikki was spooning Terri as they both watched their dad's shadow in the doorway of Omari's room. Terri looked over her shoulder at Nikki, mouth curled down, eyes wide with unknowing. Nikki saw the fright on Terri's face, rolled over on her stomach, and buried her head into the pillow.

* * *

"Sis, I remember me getting a whooping for those cookies. Man, I didn't know what was going on that night. But I wasn't surprised. Mom or Dad would always show up at my door randomly, punishing me for something they thought I did," Omari said half-jokingly and half-serious.

"I know, Brother. Nikki and I felt so bad about that. We were shamed—" Terri added before her brother interrupted her.

"Well, wh-wh-why didn't you guys speak up?" Omari asked. "I got such a bad butt whooping that night."

Terri paused, unsure of what to say.

"But seriously Sis, I didn't realize Dad terrorized Nikki that bad. And honestly, I didn't think you cared. You were so spoiled. Always acting perfect. I thought you liked us getting in trouble so you could get all the gifts and treats," Omari said.

"No, Brother. I hated when you guys got in trouble. I always thought Mom and Dad were so unfair. That's why I kept running away. I didn't have the words to express my outrage, to express my sadness, my guilt. So when it became too overwhelming, I just ran away. And when Child Protective Services came and took you away, at first I didn't know what happened. I just knew you were gone, and I was sad. I knew you were sad too, wherever you were," Terri explained as she grabbed a Kleenex to wipe her eyes and blow her nose.

"Omari, the way you were treated, the way Nikki was treated—it hurt me. It hurt me for a long time. It took years of talk therapy, meditation, and God to get me to a place where most of the thoughts from childhood can cross my mind without me getting emotional. But some incidents still bring me a bit of sadness," Terri said as she reflected on an incident with her sister and a cup of washing powder.

17

Washing Powder

NIKKI HELD HER HANDS BY HER face, palms out, guarding against an oncoming attack. She wriggled around on her back, crying out in pain and desperation.

"Mom, please get off me! Mom, please stop!" she yelled.

Calinda straddled her daughter on the large black shag sofa in the living room—the one with red fur decorating the arm rests. Calinda murmured something unrecognizable as she whaled her arms, striking Nikki anywhere she could. A hard blow landed on Nikki's torso. The afternoon light streamed through the window, casting ugly shadows on the brawl.

Nikki continued to scream. She wouldn't dare hit her mom back, but she grew weary of trying to defend her face and her body. Her cries and pleas for relief became faint with exhaustion after each blow.

Terri and her brother, Omari, tried in vain to get their mother to stop hitting their sister.

Terri, eleven years old at this point, had curled herself up in a ball and covered her ears. She shrieked, "Stop it, stop it!" as her tears fell down her now bright red cheeks. Omari sat cross-legged on the floor, rocking back and forth, tears streaming down his face as he repeatedly hit himself on the forehead with the palm of his hand. Terri felt so helpless as she watched her sister get beat and her mother lose control.

Finally, after what felt like hours, Calinda grabbed Nikki by the jaw and said, "Now, go to your goddamn room. Get out of my sight."

Nikki rolled off the couch and onto her knees. She stumbled to catch her balance as she rose to her feet and ran upstairs to her bedroom. She closed her bedroom door softly. They all knew slamming the door would just set Calinda off again.

Calinda looked over at little Terri sitting on the floor, sobbing, but she couldn't quite meet her second daughter's eyes. She stood up from her kneeled position on the couch, adjusted her shirt, ran both her hands through her thick, beautiful, chemically-straightened hair, which was now slick with sweat. She slowly walked up the stairs without saying a word.

Terri could hear the heaviness of her mother's footsteps as she walked into her own bedroom, just across the hall from Nikki's.

Hours later, Terri tapped lightly on her sister's door.

"Go away!" Nikki yelled. Terri ignored her. She carefully opened the door a crack and peeked around until her searching eyes found her sister. Nikki's body was like a limp rag doll collapsed across her bed.

"I said to go away, Peaches!" The sound of her nickname, the one given to Terri by her grandmother, made her heart ache.

"Nikki, I'm sorry you got in trouble," said Terri, still standing in the doorway.

"I didn't even do nothing!" Nikki screamed, more to herself than to her sister.

"It was me," Terri admitted with so much shame. She'd been practicing her pirouette with a cup of water in her hands and spilled it into the washing powder, rendering it totally useless. That stuff was expensive, too. But Terri was so afraid of what her mother would say to her that when she asked angrily who had spilled water in the washing powder, she'd said under her breath, "Nikki." Thinking about it now, her arms and legs felt as heavy as lead.

"Why did you tell Mom it was me?" Nikki asked. "Why did you tell a lie?"

"Oh, Nikki you know you are not supposed to say the word 'lie,'" warned Terri to deflect the real issue.

"Why did you tell a *lie*?" Nikki said even louder.

Terri took a deep breath. "I told a story because I didn't want to get in trouble, and I didn't want Mom to be mad at me."

"You are such a lying, spoiled little baby," Nikki said as she pushed herself upright on her bed. Terri could see a bruise already blooming on her cheek.

"I'm sorry, Nikki," Terri started to cry. "I am so, so sorry."

Nikki's face softened. "Come here, Peaches," she said, patting a spot on the bed next to her.

Terri began to cry uncontrollably, guilt weighing on her like a ten-ton tankard. "I made Mom hurt you," Terri said, sniffling. "I am so sorry Nikki."

Nikki put her arms around her baby sister and tried to comfort her. "It's not your fault. Mom just wanted a reason to hit me. She is crazy."

Terri continued to cry as she curled herself in a ball on her sister's bed and laid her head on Nikki's lap. "I love you, Nikki," whimpered Terri as she wiped the snot from her nose with the back of her hand.

"I love you, too. And quit touching me with that nasty, cootie-infested hand," Nikki joked, pretending to recoil from her sister.

"I'm just playing." Nikki pulled Terri in close. She held her sister as she cried, until they both fell to sleep.

When Terri woke up, the light from outside was no longer peeking through the curtains. They always ate supper as a family before it was dark outside. Terri wiggled out from under her sister's arm then shuffled downstairs, expecting to see her mother at the dinner table, angry as hell. But no one was there. She must have canceled family dinner.

Calinda was known to cancel dinner as a punishment if the kids misbehaved, usually just for the disobedient one. But sometimes, if she felt really bad, she'd cancel dinner altogether, sending everyone to bed hungry, regardless of their crime.

Terri tiptoed back to Nikki's room. Her sister was still asleep, limbs sprawled at odd angles. Terri loved her big sister, and she knew her big sister loved her too. No matter what, Nikki considered herself the protector of her younger siblings. Even when it was Nikki who needed protecting.

Terri got back into the bed and snuggled up next to her sister, and she gazed upon her face while she slept. Terri saw white chalky lines on Nikki's cheek. Terri licked her thumb, then she gently rubbed away the tear tracks. She kept caressing her sleeping sister's face even after the dried tears were gone.

Even when Terri wasn't blaming things she'd done on her sister, it seemed like Nikki was always getting grounded, getting hit, getting yelled at. But Terri couldn't understand why. Nikki seemed like a happy, normal teenager. She had a big, loud laugh and a sharp sense of humor. Admittedly, she wasn't like Terri, who always followed the rules (or seemed like she did, anyway). When Nikki found a rule unjust, she just chose not to follow it. She had her own unique brand of girl. Terri admired that about Nikki.

Nikki wanted to be a model. Terri could easily visualize her pretty, thin sister wearing a beyond glamorous gown, strutting on a runway to uproarious applause. Nikki had a beautiful smile—perfectly straight teeth even without braces. When she walked, her toes pointed outward instead of straight ahead. Calinda was always yelling at Nikki for that. On several occasions, Calinda made Nikki practice walking in the garage and onto the driveway, back and forth walking in a straight line for hours. She sometimes missed dinner because she was just not getting it right.

But Nikki desperately wanted to be a model, so she practiced and practiced. Terri remembered Calinda taking Nikki to the modeling studio to get headshots. She also took her classes on the weekends where she learned to walk and carry herself like a model. It seemed like those were the only times Calinda would show affection for her oldest daughter.

Terri would later learn that when her mother was a teenager, she had wanted to be a model too, but got pregnant with Nikki just before what could have been her big break. When it became clear her daughter was beautiful, Calinda placed her modeling dreams onto her. Nikki could be everything Calinda wasn't—and Nikki was her mirror, reflecting all of Calinda's same hopes and dreams, but also the same fears and failures. And for some reason, she just couldn't stand it.

Terri kissed her sister on the cheek, and she slid out of bed. She tiptoed across the floor as to not wake Nikki. She looked so peaceful. Terri lightly opened the door and walked across the hall to her mother's bedroom. She softly tapped on the door and whispered, "Mom, can I come in?"

"Come in, Peaches," Calinda said with a melancholy tone. Terri cracked the door and slid in and quickly closed the door behind her.

Calinda was soaking in the bathtub of the en suite surrounded by bubbles and a cloud of cigarette smoke. Terri knew her mom should not be smoking in the house—an agreement Calinda made with her family—but Terri didn't dare say anything to her now.

Terri sat on the edge of the tub. Tears welled up in her eyes.

"Mom," Terri said.

"Yes, Peaches?"

"Nikki didn't put the water in the washing powder. It was me. I spilled my cup into it when I was playing and that's why it got hard," Terri blurted out quickly, not looking at her mother.

Calinda released the smoke from her tight, pursed lips and said, "I know, Peaches. I know."

18

Military Mom

"PEACHES, DON'T LET SMOKEY JUMP ON you like that, baby," Calinda yelled out of the kitchen, her voice dripping with honey sweetness, as Terri played with one of their two Great Danes.

Calinda was preparing a gourmet meal for her family: fried shrimp tempura and a homemade fruit salad with poppy seed Dijon dressing for dipping. There was no special occasion—Calinda was just feeling good today. And when Calinda felt good, she cooked for her family. And she was a really good cook.

Luther Vandross' "A House is Not a Home" crooned on the radio as Calinda glided through the kitchen, cutting fruit and mixing sauces. The warm buttery smell of fried shrimp wafted to ten-year-old Terri's nostrils, making her mouth water. Calinda smiled and swayed her hips, grooving to the music.

Calinda was five feet, seven inches tall, with beautiful deep cocoa skin. She had naturally thick, long, brown hair she wore in a jerry curl style that day—the signature 'do of the 1980s. The pink tank top she wore read, "Don't Hate Me Because I'm Beautiful," and her slender and silky, brown arms flowed from the shoulders of the cutoff sleeves. The nails on her long elegant fingers were neatly manicured with a deep red polish. She could have been a hand model—or any kind of model for that matter. She was breathtakingly stunning when she was happy. She was whimsical and light, and that feeling was contagious. But the threat of darkness that lurked beneath her mother was hard to ignore, even in these moments of beauty and bliss.

Calinda, who grew up in poverty, had only obtained a GED. She had three failed relationships and a child to show for each. She grew up Catholic and didn't believe in abortions. And despite having three children with no fathers in sight, Calinda wanted more for her life than a life in poverty like she grew up in. She wanted the best for her children.

A few years after her youngest, Omari, was born, Calinda decided she had to get out of her mother's house, get out on her own, and get out of Detroit. There were only a few options for a young twenty-something Black woman with a GED and three children: welfare, marriage, or the military. Calinda enlisted in the Air Force at twenty-five to create a life for herself, to gain financial independence, and perhaps move her children to a new city. So Calinda left her children with her mother and set off to basic training.

Calinda was in and out of her mom's east side home on Harding Street for a couple years following her enlistment in the Air Force. When she finally returned to pick up her children, she returned with a big surprise.

When Calinda rang the doorbell of her mother's house, she stood with one arm full of gifts and the other locked around her new husband. Calinda's face glowed, her eyes danced, and she had her head held high. Calinda was back for her family, just like she said she would be. She packed up her children and headed down to Montgomery, Alabama—her next duty station.

It was in Montgomery, Alabama that Terri first remembered fearing her mother.

For the three years they lived in Montgomery, life seemed pretty happy and calm for Terri and her family. Her mom seemed content working during the day as a medical technician and taking care of her family in the evening. But Terri, Nikki, and Omari didn't have a chance to spend much time with their mom and stepdad during the week. Even without the parents around much, their household in Alabama had a *lot* of rules. They'd get home from school around 3:30 p.m., do homework or practice dictionary drills until dinner time at 5:00 p.m., and then go to bed at 6:30 p.m. *sharp*. During the week, they were not allowed to watch T.V. or go outside, and they certainly weren't allowed to have friends over. They couldn't go to the refrigerator without permission, they couldn't eat snacks without permission, and they couldn't drink anything, even water, without asking permission in advance. There was no back talk. Terri, Omari and Nikki had to address their parents as "ma'am" or "sir" at all times.

Waking up in the morning, little Terri had to make her bed with military corners, immediately brush her teeth, wash her face, and wear the clothes that were laid out for her the night before, neatly pressed with military creases. Calinda kept all her children in nice, clean, crisp clothing, their hair neatly groomed, shoes toothbrush-cleaned, and shoestrings handwashed. Calinda ran a tight ship, and her crew knew the consequences at an early age of getting out of line.

One Saturday, when Terri was eight, Terri and her family were all in the living room of their military housing on Montgomery Air Force Base watching T.V.—all but Omari, that is. Omari sat facing the corner. He had been up to regular six-year-old boy shenanigans, but in Calinda's house, those shenanigans came at a cost. Calinda dished out strict punishments for minor infractions.

On this particular day, Omari was seventeen minutes into serving his one-hour sentence of sitting in the corner, facing the wall, and decided that he wanted to use the wall as a piece of Kleenex. He smeared a juicy green booger onto the bright white wall. The next thing Terri saw was her mom's wooden clog flying across the room, hitting Omari upside the head. The force of the shoe sent Omari's head crashing against the wall, right next to the booger.

Calinda charged toward Omari, limping with just one shoe on, and picked up the clog. She whopped Omari with it again. That was the first time Terri remembered being frightened of the rage in her mother's eyes.

Years later, they moved to the next duty station in Austin, Texas. There, Calinda's rage became uncontrollable. From the outside it looked like a seemingly normal, working class family living in the suburbs, but inside of 7005 William Cannon Drive, Austin, Texas, it was a home so suffocating and strict you could not breathe without getting in trouble.

The days Calinda were happy were a big relief for Terri and her siblings. They relished in those days when their mom was gushing joy and love. As they got older those days were fewer and further between. And sometimes, they wished for just one whole day without fear.

* * *

At 5:00 p.m., after Calinda plated the shrimp tempura, Calinda called her children and husband inside to wash up for dinner. Terri and her family were excited for dinner because they loved their mom's gourmet meals. They all gathered around the large, circular glass dining room table. That night everyone was allowed to eat dinner. Eyes wide, bellies hungry, they were all laughter and giggles as they dined on the delicious, crispy shrimp.

"Nikki sit up straight! Why are you hunched over like that?

"Omari, elbows off the table! Why are you guarding your plate like that? Do you think someone will steal your food?" Calinda barked like a drill sergeant.

"Peaches, don't eat the oranges, you are allergic."

"Yes, ma'am."

19

Divergent Paths

DESPITE THE CONTROVERSIAL START OF THEIR late-night conversation, Terri and Omari had been on the phone for hours. When Terri glanced at the clock, it read 5:38 a.m., which shocked her.

"Oh my goodness, Omari, look what time it is!" Terri exclaimed.

"Sister, I did not know all of this happened. I mean I know Mom and Dad were cruel to us but some of the stories about Nikki I did not know," Omari commented.

"I know Omari, you have your own history to deal with as well. I know I don't know half the stuff you went through. I don't even know what happened to you after you went to a foster family," Terri said compassionately.

"Sis, it was so much better living with Joanna and

Bill. I didn't know families could be that happy," Omari
shared.

"Yeah, but Nikki wasn't so lucky," Terri said somberly.

Her journey was different. Her path went in the wrong
direction.

"I remember when Nikki called me from the Cross
Creek Mental Hospital. I knew at that point Nikki's life
was taking a horrible turn," Terri said, suddenly vividly
remembering that call from Nikki one week after she had
arrived in Connecticut.

* * *

Terri was nineteen when she arrived at her duty station, a
Naval Submarine Base in Groton, Connecticut, fresh out
of boot camp.

Truthfully, she'd barely made it out of boot camp. Terri
had sailed through the classroom portion, but her aver-
sion to taking orders had made the physical portion much,
much harder. Her company commander had threatened to
kick her out at least three times.

Her sensitivity and determination to do things her way
almost cost Terri her way out.

Almost.

But her company commander, Petty Officer Crutchfield,
understood Terri, as she did many of the young men
and women who come to boot camp. She knew that in
many cases, this was a person's only way out of dire

circumstances—it was their last resort. So no matter how much Terri drove Crutchfield crazy with her insubordination and independent spirit, she took compassion on Terri. Terri just needed a little structure, a little direction, a little guidance. And Crutchfield wanted to be that person to give that to young Terri. Over the thirteen weeks Terri was under her command, Crutchfield was determined to turn Terri into a buttoned-up enlisted sailor, ready to face the world.

Terri appreciated the support but hated all the extra jumping jacks she had to do every time she stepped out of line. And the jumping jacks included wearing a fully loaded sea bag on her back, suited up in her full training gearing, winter jacket, hat, complete Navy uniform, Boondockers and all. In the Navy they called this type of punishment "cycling," which meant you had to cycle through the same set of exercises, in full gear, until you either passed out with exhaustion or you made the windows sweat. The condensation on the windows usually came right before the faint. Terri must have passed out at least a half dozen times. But overtime, she began to learn the appropriate behaviors required to be an exemplary soldier.

When Terri finally turned the corner, ten pounds lighter and acting like a soldier, she landed a sweet job at the Public Affairs Office. In boot camp, that was one of the jobs to envy. Most recruits landed in the galley, which was the kitchen or outdoor cleanup duty—both very dirty, labor intensive jobs.

The sailors working in the Public Affairs Office were responsible for the flow of news and information. There, she learned about media, press releases, and journalism. When Terri signed up for the Navy, she had no idea this would be a part of it. When she began to learn about these surprising opportunities, she was endlessly glad she made the choice to join the Navy.

But when she finally made it out of boot camp, Terri was similarly glad to have made it out in one piece. She got to keep her job at the Public Affairs Office. She had a regular salary, a stable home, and nowhere to go but up. She was so excited to continue with this new chapter. A new life—one away from Detroit where Tony went to jail eight days after they were married and was sentenced to twenty-five to thirty-five years for manslaughter. Far away from 7005 William Cannon Drive in Austin, Texas, where her brother was taken by Child Protective Services and put in the foster care system, and where her sister was kicked out at just fourteen to fend for herself.

Terri had also been on her own at fourteen. Both sisters had to take complete ownership of their own lives far too soon. Both sisters were armed only with inner strength, the military-like discipline they learned from home, scars and all, and the clothes on their backs. But despite all this, Terri and Nikki's lives took very different turns. Two divergent paths.

Nikki was shuffled from group home to group home, where she was abused and sexually assaulted by the more hardened, lost girls in the shelters who were dealing with their own trauma When Nikki did manage to run away from those terrible circumstances, she had no choice but to rely on the kindness of strangers. And the strangers Nikki encountered were not so kind. Nikki started using drugs and found herself often exchanging sex for places to crash. No one offered her a helping hand; she had to beg, borrow, and steal for everything she had—not until she met Bret O'Neil.

Bret, one year younger than Nikki, fell in love the first time they met during high school. Bret and Nikki didn't date while they were in school, but after Nikki graduated, they started hanging out. When Bret graduated a year later, he moved into his own apartment, then Nikki moved in with him at nineteen. And although he loved Nikki with all his heart, and Nikki loved him, all the years of abuse, living in the streets hand to mouth, had hurt her deeper than what could be seen on the surface. She no longer had emotional safety, she no longer trusted, and her self-esteem was shattered. She needed professional support to help her unpack and heal from her past. But Nikki didn't realize that—and she wasn't about to let anyone in. Why would she? All the people from her past had hurt her. She was in constant survival mode, even with Bret.

Nikki got pregnant shortly after she moved in with him. And the shock of the sudden pregnancy at such a young age added more trauma to Nikki's already delicate mental state. She reached out to her mother when she became pregnant, and the continued criticism and judgment from Calinda only continued to push her closer to the edge.

A year after her son Kendrick was born, Nikki had a nervous breakdown. She was admitted to a psychiatric institution the very same day Terri arrived at her first duty station. While Nikki was starting a slow descent into madness, chaos, and illness, Terri's life was only just beginning.

Poem
Please Don't Let This Happen to She

Is this how the story is to be?
Please don't let this happen to she,
For she came in blameless.
Clear as a bright blue sky.

Please don't let my cloud darken her day,
Or put stumbling blocks in her way.
Please don't let this happen to she,
For she came in blameless.
Spirit full of hope and joy,
Eyes sparkling like the crisp morning dew
For she is new.

Please don't let this happen to she,
For she came in blameless.
Dreams abound and miracles to find
Blinding beauty so bright
On a path, at her feet, the light.
Please don't let this happen to she,
For she came in blameless.

Is this how the story is to be?

Part III
Was That Your Destiny?

20

Soul Mate

TERRI HEARD HER PHONE VIBRATE ON from one of her shelves in her customized California Closet as she tried on yet another pair of shoes, preparing for the day. She was launching several collaborations and one of them was helping to create a platform for little Black and Brown children to talk about themselves, their lives, and their experiences in safe spaces. She was facilitating the session that day and sometimes in her enthusiasm and excitement she would go down a stray path during her turn to speak. She had to open up this inaugural session with a few important messages. And then, in the evening, she had a date with Jean-Marc.

Terri felt a smile tug at her lips as she reached down to open the text.

Salut Terri, je viens d'arriver à l'hôtel Shinola. J'ai fait des réservations pour le dîner au San Morello Restaurant en bas. On se voit à 7 heures.

Jean-Marc had arrived in Detroit from San Francisco and was letting her know he had made dinner reservations at the Shinola Hotel for 7:00 p.m.

Terri loved when he spoke to her in his native language. Since she was just a girl, Terri had dreamed of living in France with a charming Frenchman, so she'd studied the language for two years in high school, then again to fulfill her language requirement in college. And even after she'd lived and worked in Paris, it took her ten years to find a man from France who connected with her soul.

It wasn't until Terri moved back to the States that she met the gallant French suitor of her dreams, Jean-Marc Urbain Ndedi. The son of Cameroonian immigrants, Jean-Marc had grown up in Paris and graduated from the Université Paris Sciences et Lettres before he moved to the States twenty years ago to continue his studies at the University of California in Berkeley. Jean-Marc was now a world-renowned data scientist in Silicon Valley.

Terri and Jean-Marc had met at a conference on the topic of educating young Black boys in California when Terri was there for work. They immediately connected from the moment she picked up on his French accent from across the room. He was tall and stood about six foot four. His dark brown skin and clean-shaven head glistened under the fluorescent lights of the ballroom. His slim, muscular build gave him the appearance of someone intentional about fitness and particular about his appearance. He was very well groomed with an added layer of Parisian style and sophistication that easily put Jean-Marc at the top of Terri's "Best Looking Man Ever" list. When their eyes met, it was love at first sight for Terri. She couldn't take her eyes off of him the entire two-day conference. To her delight, she noticed Jean-Marc was always looking back.

This was the first time Terri had been truly interested in a man since she and Roger. After he passed, Terri spent a long time mourning from the loss of a love that helped her transform her life. Still, she continued on her healing journey, focusing on her personal and professional development.

Terri was optimistic about love and about life. She had overcome so many challenges in her life and seen so much tragedy. She was grateful to be healthy, happy, whole, and pursing her passions. She knew at the right time God would send her a soul mate. As Terri glanced back down at the text, blushing, she knew she had found that in Jean-Marc. But they were only a few months into their romance and were still getting to know each other. There were so many similarities in their childhood, in their parenting journey, and in their vision for making a difference for young Black boys and girls.

Because of both of their journeys, they knew how resilient all little Black boys and girls were if only given access to some of the same educational opportunities, resources, and support they had. They understood that talent is equally distributed among all children, no matter the race—but opportunity was not. Little Black and Brown boys and girls needed advocates, champions, and change agents to fight to make sure there was equity, no matter their situation.

As Terri finally decided on the *perfect* pair of nude patent leather Louboutins that would work well both for her work presentation that day and her dinner with Jean-Marc that evening, Terri recalled their very first date. It was still so vivid in Terri's memory. Over dinner was when she revealed so much of her childhood to him. Things she had only ever shared with Roger and the counselors.

Terri's recollection of their first date conversation was so intense, just the memory brought tears to her eyes, blurring her vision as she swiped a hot pink Chanel shade onto her lips. She set the tube onto the counter, then grabbed for either side with trembling hands. She took a deep breath, and was drawn back into the conversation where she had explained why she ran away from home at fourteen. She shared how that past came to a climax while she was working in Paris. How her past and present collided in Paris and changed her life trajectory completely . . .

21

Healing Journey

WHEN TERRI TOLD JEAN-MARC HER STORY over dinner at La Folie, a high-end French restaurant near the conference center, he sat quietly in the elegant, vintage, arm chair across from hers, very focused on every word Terri was saying. Terri liked that about Jean-Marc—he was present, always.

"Terri, I am so amazed, given everything you've experienced, you have so much joy! You are so radiant and full of hope," he said. "How do you do that?"

Without a beat Terri said, "God."

Jean-Marc nodded in agreement. "Absolument," he said in French. As an ordained minister who'd obtained his master's in divinity when he first arrived in Berkley, Jean-Marc was a man of faith.

"Isn't God transformational?" he asked, full of wonder at God's power.

"Yes, God and years of therapy," Terri said with a smile.

Terri had learned to be very comfortable acknowledging the importance therapy played in her life. Therapy helped her problem solve, it helped her overcome anxiety, it helped her breakthrough her depression. She was grateful. The counseling and support she received prompted her to obtain her master's degree in social work with a concentration in children, youth, and families. Part of the work she was doing with young Black and Brown children was inspired by one particular therapist she had in the Navy.

As she told her story to Jean-Marc, she remembered her first encounter with therapy . . .

* * *

Terri's mom tried to get her to see a therapist the first time Terri had truly tried to run away from home. Terri had packed one of her mom's big blue suitcases and got a Greyhound bus ticket to Detroit, where she'd stay with Mother Dear. But before she could board the bus, she was detained by security at the station.

Terri had sat in a small, windowless room the officers had locked her in for several hours, arms covered in goose bumps, her entire body shivering—partly from the blasting air conditioner and partly with fear. When her mom finally arrived, Terri immediately burst into tears and started apologizing. But her mom wasn't angry, she was rather very empathetic. Calinda knew there was a lot going on with Terri, and in many ways she felt guilty for that. A piece of Calinda knew she wasn't doing a good job raising a family. She had already lost two children, and she was scared of losing Terri, too. She told Terri she needed to see a psychologist to work out her emotions, which was a lesson learned from the handling of Terri's siblings. Terri went to a couple sessions but didn't really open up. The only time the therapist would get a word out of Terri was when there was food involved. The therapist would bribe Terri by taking her to the Schlotzsky's downstairs in the lobby of her office, and Terri *loved* Schlotzsky sandwiches. Mouth full, she would share a bit more, but not much. After a few sessions, Calinda decided it wasn't worth the money if Terri wasn't ready to discuss her feelings.

Terri had tried to run away countless times before, usually to her best friend Tyesha's house. Calinda always knew where to find her. Terri *wanted* her mom to find her. Running away was to test her mother's love. If she came, she'd prove, in Terri's mind, that her mother loved her.

But this run—this getaway—this escape was different. Terri didn't want to be found. She wanted to get as far away from her mother as possible. She was *so* angry, so hurt, so helpless over Calinda forcing Nikki out of the house to go live in a girls' home. Her brother, Omari, was taken by Child Protective Services and put into foster care. Now, at twelve-years-old, Terri found herself alone.

After her siblings were gone, Calinda separated from K.C. She moved herself and Terri into a two-bedroom apartment nearby. Calinda worked nights at the IRS, which left Terri alone on the weeknights with the same strict rules that applied in their old house. Terri had to come straight home from school every day to walk their giant, shiny black Great Dane named Smokey. That part Terri loved; Smokey was one of her best friends.

After she walked Smokey, she had to cook dinner for herself. And even though her mom always made sure the pantry and fridge were stocked with stuff to make tacos, Terri's favorite meal, Terri was still sad that she had to eat alone, with the exception of Smokey; she fed him tacos too.

She had a desk in her bedroom that faced a window that overlooked the apartment building's parking lot. As she sat and did her homework, she could see all the other kids outside, playing and goofing around. But she had to do homework and be in the bed by 8:00 p.m. No excuses. Sometimes Terri's mom would pop in on her lunch break just to make sure Terri was in bed on time or to make sure she wasn't sneaking out of the house or to make sure she wasn't watching T.V. Despite how frustrated she was with her mother's tyrannical reign, Terri almost always complied. Even so, Calinda had enlisted a neighbor, Diana, across the breezeway to be a lookout. That kept Terri in line for a little while, but once her mom fell out with Diana, Terri was free to roam.

Terri was bored being there at night by herself and

lonely. She had been lonely even before she'd moved out with her mother. When they'd all lived together, her brother and sister seemed to always be in trouble for something, confined to their rooms or to sitting in some random corner of the house facing the wall on punishment.

And even when Calinda was home and off work, her mom would have dates.

Calinda was distracted with all the men in her life, and because she was always trying to better herself by working hard and taking classes, she didn't focus much of her energy on Terri.

Calinda hadn't graduated from high school and had always regretted that and wanted to better herself. That ambition coupled with the disappointment of not continuing her education obsessed her. On more than one occasion, Calinda would tell Terri how Terri and her siblings had ruined her life. It was because of them she didn't have a career. Those words cut like a knife. They made Terri feel like a burden and turn a cold heart toward her mom.

Terri resented her mom for her unkind words, but even more for her abusive and hurtful actions toward her brother and sister, all of which Terri had, for some reason, been spared from. Terri did not know why she was spared from the torrent of terror, but either way, she held a grudge—a hurt, and deep emotional wounds she would carry with her throughout her young adult life—and throughout much her motherhood.

Terri was in ninth grade when she finally ran away from home for good. She remembered the last question she asked her mom before she left.

"Mom, are you going to pay for me to go to college?"

Calinda responded, "I don't have money to send you to college." At that moment, Terri decided there was no benefit to her staying any longer. She felt she would rather take a chance on her own to see what she could create out of her life for herself. Days later, Terri ran away from home once and for all. And this time, her mother didn't follow.

Terri knew she was carrying some heavy emotional baggage with her. And she wanted to be more of a mother than her mom. When Terri arrived at her first duty station years later, she sought out therapy.

22

Somehow, She Knew

TERRI CONTINUED TO SHARE HER CHILDHOOD experiences with Jean-Marc as they grew closer over several months. She had spent the past fifteen years unpacking her childhood. Therapy was a resource that gave her the emotional strength to handle what lay ahead and open up to Jean-Marc, who always listened.

As Terri began to share more of her life with Jean-Marc over the course of their relationship, she remembered her last encounter with her sister ...

* * *

Terri heard banging—the dual sounds of thunder and a knock on her door seemed to shake the apartment.

"Nikki? Nikki is that you?" called Terri.

She pulled herself up from where she slept on the couch, straining her neck to get a view of the door. The sofa in Terri's Paris flat was positioned so she couldn't see the front door from her living room. The space was cozy, forty square meters in the center of Paris near Jardin des Tuileries, which Queen Catherine de Medici built in 1564 and was re-landscaped under King Louis XIV. It was smaller than she was used to now, but the garden more than made up for this minor inconvenience. However, the condensed floor configuration did mean she could not see who was at the door.

She heard the door open and close and the unmistakable sound of her sister's model sashay. She'd recognize those footsteps anywhere.

"Nikki?"

But Nikki didn't answer. Terri saw her sister walk into her kitchen and sit on a barstool in the kitchen nonchalantly, as if she, not Terri, owned the place.

"Nikki, is that you?" Terri rose a little higher, trying to meet her sister's gaze. She kept calling her name, but Nikki remained silent. Suddenly, there was a bolt of lightning, and with a swift turn of the neck, Nikki turned her face toward Terri. In the split-second flash, Terri could see it was not her sister perched at the counter. It was a dark figure in a hooded cloak. Terri screamed and fell off her couch onto the hardwood floors.

With a sharp intake of breath, Terri bolted upright

on her couch. Her shirt, soaked with sweat, clung to her back. She clutched her chest, trying to regain control of her breath. She looked around—there was no storm, no hooded figure, just Terri.

"It was just a dream," Terri said to herself as she tried to steady herself. Her mind was reeling. What did the silent hooded figure have to do with her sister? Nikki had disappeared eight years ago without a trace, leaving her three young children without their mother. Neither Terri nor her children had heard from her since.

Then Terri's phone vibrated beneath a pillow on the couch, which startled Terri all over again.

"Jesus Christ," Terri yelled angrily as she whacked the couch pillow with her fist. Terri snatched her phone from the couch spooked, frustrated, and tired.

She tapped the phone and when the screen lit up she saw she had seven missed calls from her twenty-one-year-old nephew in Austin—Kendrick, Nikki's son. They had just spoken last night. While Kendrick called Terri often in search of advice or when he needed some money, he never called two days in a row. Looking at the log of missed calls, Terri could sense his frantic energy.

Something was wrong.

Nikki, Terri thought to herself.

Terri quickly dialed Kendrick back without listening to his string of voicemails, her heart in her throat. He answered on the second ring.

"Aunt Terri?"

"What is it, Kendrick?"

There was a tense, quiet moment that felt like an eternity.

"My mom is dead," Kendrick whimpered.

Terri let the phone fall to her lap, then out came an uncontrolled shriek. "No!" she cried.

She knew she should keep it together for the sake of her nephew, but this pain, this *noise,* flew from her body like angry ghosts. It wouldn't stop.

She knew one day this call would come. She just didn't think it would be *now.* This was the climax of Nikki's entire life story—a life of being brutally punished at the hands of her parents at every turn.

She was heartbroken at the news that came from Kendrick, the oldest of Nikki's children, still so young with so much weight on his shoulders. Terri hastily tried to comfort him, but she needed to know what happened.

"Oh my God, Kendrick, I am so sorry. What happened? How do you know?" She felt she was operating at warped speed.

"I got a call from her boyfriend in Detroit—"

"Nikki was in Detroit?" Terri interrupted.

"Apparently," Kendrick said somberly. "Her boyfriend said she hanged herself."

There it was again—the pain embodied in sound. Terri shrieked as tears rolled down her cheeks.

"She . . . she hanged herself?"

"While her boyfriend was at work. When he came home,

he found her in the basement." Kendrick was now sobbing on the other line. Both Terri and Kendrick cried on the phone. They sobbed and sobbed until Terri's head began to ache.

"Auntie, what do we do now?" he said.

"We're going to Detroit. You and me. You don't have to handle it by yourself, Kendrick."

"I have to get up there now," he said with the utmost sense of urgency. "I've found a couple plane tickets out of Austin tomorrow. I can be in Detroit by tomorrow evening."

"Sounds like you've come up with a good plan, Sweetheart," Terri tried to comfort him while slowing him down just long enough for her to wrap her head around what was happening. "Let's go through your plan to make sure I can get a flight out of Paris and meet you at the airport in Detroit, okay, love?"

"Okay."

"Listen, I know you have been up all night. Try to get some rest, give me a couple hours. I'll be there. I love you, Kendrick," Terri said trying to comfort her nephew.

"I love you too, Auntie," Kendrick said softly.

Terri hung up the phone. Her head and shoulders suddenly became too heavy to hold up. She slumped over and curled up into tight ball on her couch. Tears streaming down the side of her face as she felt hot liquid fill her ear. The pain was no longer a sound but an overwhelming ache that enveloped her entire body.

When she closed her eyes, all she could see was her sister at fourteen, slim and frightened, holding a large, green garbage bag on the front porch of 7005 William Cannon Drive. Terri was only twelve at the time, but somehow, she knew Nikki wasn't going to be all right.

Somehow, she knew this day, this call, this heartbreak would come.

Somehow, she knew.

23

No Show

"CALINDA, IT'S YOUR FAULT NIKKI IS dead!" Terri screamed into her phone at her mother with the same tangible rage and sorrow she felt when Kendrick had told her the news of her sister's death. She could feel the agony in her throat and chest.

Calinda had not shown up to the funeral of her first born.

Terri was so angry and so filled with disgust, she did not acknowledge Calinda as her mother anymore. She didn't deserve the respect of that title. Mothers were supposed to nurture and offer unconditional love, and yet Calinda shirked every responsibility, leaving her daughter to die. Terri knew that calling Calinda by her first name would send her through the roof.

But this was just a voicemail. Terri pictured her mother, staring at her phone as it rang and rang, too full of too much cowardice to pick it up. Terri left a voicemail filled with so much rage and venom that she would one day deeply regret leaving it. But when she first hung up the phone, she felt like she had finally stood up to her mother, expressing all the emotions that she had only shared with her therapist. She never wanted to say these things directly to her mother, because she always feared hurting her mother's feelings. Terri knew her mother wasn't mentally, emotionally, or spiritually strong enough to face all the pain she'd caused her children. But today, the day she couldn't even show up for Nikki's funeral, Terri didn't care about her mother's feelings.

Immediately after the funeral, Terri and her old friend Kimi drove over to the green four-bedroom house on William Cannon Drive where Terri and her siblings were terrorized. After Terri ran away, Calinda fell ill and moved back in with K.C. Both Calinda and K.C. still lived there. When she was growing up, the house had to be kept immaculate, especially on the outside. They had to keep up appearances for the neighbors. The grass was always freshly cut and flower gardens painstakingly manicured. Terri remembered hours of her and Nikki picking out weeds one-by-one.

But now, it didn't even look like the same house. The grass was overgrown, the bushes all out of sorts, and the garage door facing the street was rotting and falling off its hinges. This was the worst looking house on the upscale, suburban block flanked by white picket fences.

Terri walked slowly up the broken concrete stairs to the porch. She took a deep breath and rang the doorbell. Minutes went by. She rang again—another unanswered chime. But she saw K.C.'s old pickup in the drive—they had to be home. Terri rang again and again, then began pounding on the door with closed fists. Then she screamed.

And screamed.

And screamed.

Terri screamed and banged until she exhausted herself. She fell to her knees and wept.

All the memories, all the pain of her childhood came flooding back to Terri. Her mind was racing, her heart beating so fast. She thought she was having a nervous breakdown. This was the porch where she saw her fourteen-year-old sister holding a garbage bag of clothes on her way to a group home. That was the beginning of the end for Nikki. Once she entered the group home, she shut herself off to love and support completely. And now things had come full circle. Terri was on the same porch, her sister dead. Her sister *dead*. Gone forever.

Terri would never again hear Nikki's infectious laugh. Or see that mischievous Nikki smile. Or hear those wonderful Nikki wise cracks. Or feel that special big sister love. Her heart was broken. And it was all Calinda's fault.

Kimi just sat next to her and allowed her to express her grief, her sorrow, her anger, her heartache.

"It's okay Terri. Cry, curse—do whatever you need right now," said Kimi.

"Why wouldn't they come to Nikki's funeral? Their own daughter!" Terri sobbed. "They are so selfish. I hate them!"

Terri pounded her fist on the splintered porch, splitting the skin on her knuckles.

"Calinda, it's your fault Nikki's dead! You and K.C. mistreated her when she was just an innocent girl. No child should receive bloody noses and bruised ribs from their parents. No child should get punched or have arms twisted behind their backs, no matter what they've done wrong. Nobody's child should be forced to eat packages of Oreos until they puke just because they snuck cookies in the middle of the night. No little girl should be beaten by a grown-ass man. And nobody's baby should ever get put out on the street at fourteen. But you did this to Nikki. You did this to Nikki and now she's dead! Now she is gone forever! And you didn't even have the balls to come to her funeral. I hate you! I wish you were dead."

24

A Familiar Number

TERRI JOLTED AWAKE WITH A PIT in her stomach. She had once again fallen asleep on her living room couch while watching BBC World News. Terri pried her heavy eyelids open to orient herself to where she was and the time of day.

"Okay, I'm in my flat," Terri said to herself.

She often had to do these kinds of pulse checks since she traveled so much for work. One week she was in Milan, then in Amsterdam the next. Just last week she had traveled to Russia. Her amazing career took her all over the globe. Terri loved this international lifestyle, her high-profile status as an executive of a global luxury fashion house, and the adventure of learning various languages. She felt blessed she was able to use her resilience and tenacity as a young runaway to persevere, navigate, and dominate in the corporate arena. God had put so many people in her path to help her along the way. He opened doors for her that could only be opened by divine intervention. He had consoled her and guided her when she fell. But through all her challenges, Terri made it. She made it! And although extremely grateful, there was something missing. She felt like she had a larger calling in her life.

Terri remembered laying across her bed the day before she ran away from home for good at fourteen. Out of nowhere, there had been a voice, an inner prompting that said, "Terri, you will do great things in this lifetime."

A chill had run up her spine. She was frightened. What *was* that voice? A spirit? A thought? She had been home alone at the time, no one near to confide in. She had called her dog Smokey into the bedroom for comfort.

As an adult, Terri often reflected on that moment. She did feel like she could achieve greatness, but she wasn't sure if it would be at Louis Vuitton, the corporate company she worked for. She was on track to become the next president of the brand, but the thought of that didn't excite her. In fact, she found the thought to be quite boring. *Is this it?* she wondered.

Terri had been grappling with this feeling for the past couple years. Once she was promoted to VP of Strategy, she felt like she had accomplished all she wanted in the corporate world. But even once she had accomplished this goal, she felt she wanted to do something more meaningful with her life. She remembered her passion for social justice when she was an undergrad at the University of Michigan. She had been a political science major taking graduate level courses in race, politics, and social justice. She interned for the father of Environmental Justice, Dr. Bunyan Bryant and State Senator Alma Wheeler, a strong proponent of education reform. She was a member of the Black Action Movement. She was even president of the Black Pre-Medical Society (although after her run-in with organic chemistry, it was made clear medicine was not her calling).

Terri wanted to fight for change.

Months after her sister's death, she recalled the passion, purpose, and commitment she had for making the lives of young Black people better.

When her college mentor, Roy, asked her once after class what she wanted to do with the rest of her life, she had said, "I want to run for office and I want my platform to be education reform." But Roy threw a bucket of cold water on her dreams.

"Look, Terri. I think you would make an awesome politician. I could even see you as Mayor of Detroit, Governor of Michigan—Terri I could see you as the Secretary of Education! You are so talented you could do anything you want."

"Thank you," Terri had responded. "I think so, too ... that's exactly what I want to do!"

"However—"

"However? Why don't you support my dreams?" Terri had interrupted with a very disappointed tone, folding her arms to her chest. "You said I can do anything."

"Hold on Terri," he'd chuckled.

"Okay, but—"

"Terri, listen to me," he said, trying not to dash young Terri's spirits. "You are a single parent with a young daughter," he'd said.

Terri rolled her eyes in disbelief.

She thought this man believed in her—he was the one who told her she could do anything. He was the one who told her to dream big. He was the one who told her she was the smartest young lady he had ever met. And now he was chastising her for being a young single mother?

He'd looked at Terri's defensive body language and patiently stayed on message. "You need to make some money first, Terri. You need a career that will provide for you and Zoe. You said you wanted to give Zoe the best education, experiences, the best life. The only way to do that is to make a little money."

Terri's face had softened as she realized her mentor *did* believe in her. Not only that, he was thinking about Zoe. Zoe was the reason Terri pushed so hard. She had to give Zoe a bright future. Set her up for success in life. She wanted Zoe to have a better start than she had. She wanted to open the world up for Zoe in a way it wasn't as open to her.

"Look into management consulting with the Big Five, the top five global consulting firms in the world, or investment banking with some of the best firms on Wall Street. They come on campus to recruit every year," said Roy. "You have the head for business, Terri, and you could make $50,000 to $90,000 coming out of undergraduate."

The numbers stunned Terri. She could hardly picture that kind of money. "Whoa, really?"

"Then once you get a few years' experience under your belt, go back to school, get you a Master of Business Administration from a top-tier graduate school, and in five years you will be making six figures."

Terri's mind was exploding and her eyes were dancing with excitement.

She had not thought of business as a career path. Luckily, her mentor was a successful, wealthy Black entrepreneur. He helped her expand her world, expand her possibilities, expand her imagination.

Terri credits Roy, in part, for her career now. If it wasn't for him, she may not have taken the business path. And although not fulfilled with her career, she was so grateful for the experience the corporate life had given her.

Suddenly, Terri's phone began to buzz, running wild across the hardwood floor. She picked up the phone and immediately recognized her home number from 7005 William Cannon Drive. It was her mom and stepdad.

Terri's eyebrows furrowed. She had not heard from her mom since Terri had left the horrible voicemail after Nikki's funeral. She'd called again to apologize, but once again, was sent to voicemail.

She was scared to answer the phone. She knew it had to be her mom. Her stepdad never called her, especially if Mom was mad at her.

It had to be Calinda. And if Calinda was calling after months of silence, Terri knew she was in for an earful. Calinda had a way with words and when she was happy, her voice was filled with sweetness and laughter, but both were rare as each year passed. When she was in a bad mood, she could be cold, manipulative, belittling, and dismissive. Even after all these years, Calinda had a special gift of stirring up guilt in Terri—in all her kids. She played the victim very well.

But Terri, not Peaches, was an adult now. Even though it was quite challenging and still a bit scary, she learned how to guard her heart against her mother's attacks. Terri learned that children should never be blamed for ruining their parents' lives. It took years of talk therapy for Terri to internalize that fact. But she had and she had also learned to stand up for herself and her brother and her sister.

Terri looked at the phone, took a deep breath, and steadied herself. "Hello?"

"Terri, this is your father."

25

Surrender

TERRI IMMEDIATELY DROPPED THE PHONE AND burst into tears. K.C. never called Terri. I mean, *never*.

Terri knew, in that moment, that her mother was dead. The same audible grief that swelled when she got the news about Nikki surged again and she yelled.

It was July twenty-third—one day after her mother's birthday and six months after Nikki had taken her own life. Terri was still grieving her sister's death, and her sorrow now compounded.

The last words she had said to her mother were, "I wish you were dead." Even though Terri followed that up with an apology message days later, she still felt the words weigh heavy on her heart.

What Terri had come to finally realize, after a long

journey of seeking God, support, and healing, is that her mother deserved compassion. She finally realized how hard her mother had to fight. How hard she had tried to create a life for her children. How hard it was for Calinda to carry the weight and the trauma of her own brokenness. Calinda's developmental wounds were never addressed or healed from her own childhood when her mother left her with her abusive father. A childhood where her father sexually abused Calinda and her sisters. He'd almost broken her, but Calinda was determined to move beyond her hurt. She was determined to be bigger than her circumstances, to not let her situation define her.

What took Terri more than twenty years to learn is how far her mother had to stretch to give her kids a fighting chance. She tried to create the home she wished she had when she was young, but the only models of happy families Calinda saw were on T.V. shows. She wanted a house in the nice suburbs. A flower garden full of beauty and splendor. A vegetable garden abundant with all the nutrients her children needed to grow. Two Great Danes and a picket fence. Three healthy, hot meals a day for her children. Clean, pressed clothes for her babies. Kids who spoke and behaved properly, armed to face a world that would judge them by the color of their skin. Calinda had worked so hard to build the dream, and she went as far as her resilient, brilliant, beautiful broken spirit could take her.

But the stressors that came along with parenthood became too great. They eventually became too overwhelming for Calinda, especially as her children grew older. And Nikki, with a mind of her own and an independent spirit, presented a challenge for Calinda. And Omari—when it came to him, she had no idea what to do with a young Black boy who couldn't quite fit in, no matter how hard she pushed him, no matter how violently she punished him.

The guilt crippled her. She'd given up on her son, drove one daughter away, and abandoned the other. And now one daughter was dead. All the emotions came crashing down onto Calinda in a final tidal wave. A tidal wave of self-surrender. An escape from the guilt, the shame, and the unforgiveness of self. A hope for rest from the inability to find peace, to find joy, to find healing, to seek support.

26

Blessed Life

TERRI HAD TOLD ALL OF THIS—the stories of Nikki and of Calinda—to Jean-Marc within their first few dates. Now, still standing in the bathroom of her Detroit home, she rolled her eyes, shook her head, and cupped her face. She couldn't believe she shared her complete family history with Jean-Marc so soon.

"I wonder if it was too much?" she asked herself out loud. She sighed. "God, what did I do?" she said, looking up at the vaulted ceiling of her house.

"Okay, Terri. Take a breath, it's okay," she told herself. If he had flown all the way to Detroit, then all hope wasn't lost. They hadn't known each other all that long—just two months—but Terri didn't want to let him slip away.

Still, she was nervous. Terri pulled out her brown

leather journal, the one she used every morning for meditation for the past twenty years. She had it restored umpteen times and had a stockpile of page refills in her study. She loved this journal; it was the first lavish gift she was able to purchase for herself in her twenties.

Whenever Terri needed comfort, she journaled her feelings to God, always starting with gratitude.

Dear God,

Thank you for this day. Thank you for my health, my family, and a warm place to rest my head. Thank you for your daily guidance, direction, protection. Thank you for being my comforter. You are awesome!

God, I have two big things on my mind this evening. The first being the work I am doing on your behalf.

Thank you for choosing me to help your Brown and Black children Lord. I believe the work I am doing is my destiny. It's my purpose for being here. My purpose for waking up each day is to help your children, O Lord. I am grateful for my wonderful life, God. Please continue to bless me so I can continue to bless others, Father. There is so much I want to do for our children, for our families, for our communities. Thank you for putting the right people in my path and creating the right situations to help me do your good work.

God, second, I don't know if I shared too much information with Jean-Marc yesterday. I really believe he is my soul mate, and that you sent him to me. And God, if he is my soul mate, he needs to know me. Who I am, what made me, me. It was important for me to let him know it was my sister's death and then my mother's death that prompted me to change careers and come back to the States, to help little boys and girls so they can be okay speaking out about their hard situations. To know it's okay to ask for help. I want them to know they can take control of their destiny and no matter what happened to them they are beautiful, brilliant, and resilient. And it's because of my life, my sister's life, my mother's life and death, that I do this work. And it was important for me to share that with Jean-Marc. If he was meant for me, that won't scare him. In fact, he will be proud of the woman I am. Thank you Lord for helping me realize that.

I love you,
Terri

Feeling comforted, confident, and energized by her journaling, Terri continued preparing for her events of the day. She moved into her home office, sat at her desk, grabbed her pink notepad, and began preparing for the launch of "Let's Talk," a program she was hosting. "Let's Talk" was a forum Terri had created as a platform to give young boys and girls space to express themselves. It was geared toward young people experiencing trauma. Much of the work Terri did on behalf of young Black and Brown children was inspired by her own life and the help and support she wished her—and more importantly her siblings—could have received when they were living through abuse. On her notepad she wrote, "It is our role as little Black Detroit girls to support our little Black Detroit boys. It is our role as little Black Detroit boys to support our little Black Detroit girls... It is our role as grown Black Detroit women and grown Black Detroit men, to uplift and support each other and to reach out, reach back, and lift up all little Black and Brown Detroit children..."

In the middle of her thoughts, a gentle chime rang from the foyer. Her heart leapt. Jean-Marc was here to pick her up for dinner. Terri floated to the front door already elegantly dressed in her Hugo Boss Pale Pink Belted Dress and opened it. There stood Jean-Marc, tall and handsome in a stunning Armani tuxedo, holding a dozen long stem roses.

"Bonjour, Mon Ami," he said as he handed her the beautifully fragrant bouquet of flowers.

"Bonjour," Terri said with her best French pronunciation and wide Terri grin.

In a very poised and gallant manner, Jean-Marc knelt onto one knee, pulled a beautiful small Tiffany blue box out of his right tuxedo pant pocket and said with his charming French accent, "Terri, will you do me the honor of allowing me to love you for the rest of my life?"

"Oui, Jean-Marc," Terri said, so full of love.

Jean-Marc wiped away the tear drops from her hand, slid the ring on her long, elegant finger, looked up to meet her eyes and said, "I love you—all of you."

Poem
Was That Your Destiny?

Two born of the same maternity.
Two born with the same destiny.
Light was there, too dim to see,
Lost and hopeless, too dark to see,
Alone and abandoned, too hard to be.
Your life you gave, my light you saved.
My life you saved, my road you paved.
Was that your destiny?
And now my journey?
To use my life, to give the light
The road I pave, for those I save.
Is that my destiny?
Is that why you saved me?

About the Author

Dr. Erica Robertson was a little Black Detroit girl who ventured out nationally and internationally to learn, explore, and grow. She has returned to her hometown to help break the cycles of intergenerational poverty by disrupting the systems that perpetuate trauma and education inequities in our Brown and Black communities.

To achieve this transformational agenda, Dr. Robertson currently serves as CEO of Promise Schools Charter Management Organization, radically reimagining the PreK 12 education landscape in Detroit, Michigan. She is the Founder of Education at Scale Foundation, a national non-profit organization focused on education equity, and is the Owner of Little Black Girl Adventures Publishing, which specializes in creating platforms for young writers of color to share their voice on a world stage. Dr. Robertson is committed to inspiring, promoting, and developing positive self-identity, healing, happiness, and togetherness in our young Black and Brown boys and girls.

🐦 📷 @lilblackdetgirl
🌐 littleblackdetroitgirl.com